Hydroponics

GN01017643

A Beginners Guide to Set Up anu ιντιιι.....
Sustainable Organic Hydroponic-System.

By

Thomas Watergreen

Table of contents

Introduction

What is Hydroponics?

As a subset of hydroculture, hydroponics grows plants in a wholly aquatic environment. This means that there's no soil, ever. For anyone who loves both innovation and gardening, it's the perfect hobby to tinker with. For those concerned about their family's food safety, it's the ideal way to make sure the food they eat is healthy and free of commercial pesticides. It's a modern way of growing that uses artificial lighting and a nutrient solution to ensure that plants have the ideal growing environment. Since you're in control of everything, you can grow your favorite plants anywhere.

Benefits of Hydroponics

As a vast industry that's becoming more popular with the general public, hydroponics has plenty of benefits. It allows people to grow plants outside of their regular season and in environments that would otherwise not be suitable. It's a great way to adapt land that may have become over-farmed or be unsuited thanks to drought or toxicity. Commercial hydroponics is relatively mainstream, and while there's a lot of stigmas thanks to the cannabis industry, it's something that is going to become increasingly popular as good farming land becomes less available, and food demand rises.

Grow Year-Round

Thanks to being an indoor project, you're not limited by the time of year. Many temperate or even arid climates will not support farming outside year-round. This means that you can grow fresh crops year-round without being at the whim of Mother Nature, and it also means your crops are safe from environmental disasters like river pollution and acid rain.

Better Plants

Since you have complete control over your plant's nutritional needs, you can grow them to the best of their ability. You know your plant has enough of everything to grow bigger and better than any soil version could. You'll have a higher yield because your plant is healthier and can physically produce more.

Environmentally Friendly

Hydroponics actually uses 2/3 less water than conventional farming since you're recirculating the water and not letting it runoff. This also means that if there is ever an accident and the water becomes hazardous, it's again not merely running into the local environment. Damaging the ecosystem like traditional farming methods often does. This also means it's not as expensive since you're not using as much water or as many nutrients because they're recirculated, and it's more efficient.

Enjoyable

Soil farming is backbreaking work. Whether it's kneeling down to put plants in or tilling the soil, traditional gardening means physical work. Since you're not doing any of these things and your plants are grown at table height, you can enjoy it more. It's also an excellent scientific method that provides an exciting project for the whole family. Most kids hate getting into the garden but tell them to start mixing solutions that change color and monitoring things to see how they grow, and it becomes much more interactive.

Are there Disadvantages?

Even though there's plenty of reasons to choose hydroponics, many shy away from this "new" technology just because it's unfamiliar or because of the stigmatic connection with cannabis growing.

The most significant factor for most people is that the initial investment is costly. Dirt is merely cheap, especially when compared to grow beds, special monitors, lighting, and the time needed to get everything running right. An extensive system is incredibly daunting as no one wants to make that sort of investment and then find it's not going to work for them.

The only real disadvantage to hydroponics is that it is a delicate system. One failure and the entire crop can be ruined in a matter of hours. No matter what medium you choose, if the water stops flowing, your plants will dry out quickly and die. Similarly, the wrong concentration of water and your plants will starve. It requires constant monitoring and commitment, something that with most people busy lives, they just can't see themselves doing.

So why would you choose it?

Well, the fact that you can produce bigger, better, and more productive than any other method speaks for itself. Your extra care will yield different results. Once you have the hang of the basics and your system set up, the running costs are relatively minimal in comparison. If you're daunted, simply start small and go from there.

Types of Hydroponic Systems

The ideal hydroponic system creates the perfect environment for plants to thrive. It's designed around their needs. There's no specific correct way to develop a structure as long as it's arranged in such a way that your plants get enough water and nutrients without rotting. At the end of the day, it's merely pumping liquid over the roots and how you want to arrange it.

The Basics

Plants need certain things to survive, and 5 essential elements need to be catered to if you want that to happen:

☐ Location

☐ Space

☐ Light

☐ Protection

☐ Warmth

Location

When starting hydroponics, you probably already have a space in mind. It can be indoors or outdoors provided you can provide a suitable environment for plant growth. For example, what happens in winter if you're growing outside? Do you plan to stop, or are you going to create some form of shelter? While it's not as essential that you monitor the system frequently like an aquaponics arrangement, things can still go wrong, so is it somewhere you can get to check on it? Does it have water and electricity access to keep everything running, right? You'll want to have your system somewhere that isn't getting disturbed, and away from children, so they don't get into the chemicals and fertilizers.

Space

The great thing about hydroponics is that you don't need soil, so you can literally grow anywhere. It's also easy to fit a hydroponic system into a small space since you can arrange your plants vertically.

When you're starting out, it's a common accident to try and fill the entire space but start out with a simple system and then build on that way, you'll be better able to understand how to allocate your space best.

As you add more elements, it can get more expensive since you'll need more nutrients and a bigger pump. The first step in any hydroponic setup is to decide precisely where you want to put in – a location with access to water and electricity at a minimum.

It's not just choosing the right space that's essential plants also need enough room for them to grow. The plant's leaves are where it breathes atmospheric gases, and without these gases, it can't grow. If the plants are too cramped, there aren't enough space or gas molecules to breathe correctly, which can stunt their growth.

Light

Plants need sunlight or artificial light that imitates sunlight, which means it has to have the right spectrum of light rays for plants to photosynthesize. Most plants want between 2-6 hours a day of strong sunlight at a minimum, but some species prefer as much as 18 hours if they're going to flourish. Unless you want to grow outside, you're going to need artificial lighting, which can get expensive. Artificial lights also get quite hot, and this can be overwhelming for the plants and a dangerous fire hazard. It's a basic you really can't skimp on, though.

Protection

Your plants will want a specific ambient temperature to flourish. If you live in extreme heat or cold or have scorching lights, you'll want to be able to monitor and adjust so they don't die.

Apart from extreme temperatures allowing rainwater to get into your system can screw up your pH and nutrient balance, plus it can dilute the water, so your plants aren't getting the nutrients they need.

The pH balance can be a real issue with some sensitive species, and wild swings can easily damage their roots. Wind will also cause the water in your system to evaporate much faster, so you want as little water exposed to the air as possible. Taller plants will also need to be supported if there's any chance of wind to prevent them from snapping.

Warmth/cool

If your system is outside you, need to expect temperature swings and realistically be able to maintain an average temperature around what is ideal for your plants. It's pretty easy to gauge the local climate with weather apps and internet info so you can decide what the maximum is or minimum you can grow at. You may find that certain seasons are totally unsuited for growing anything outside because it's simply too cold. In an indoor setup, you don't have to worry about this, and you'll only have small fluctuations to deal with. Some plants are hardier than others and can withstand colder temperatures, which means you should consider switching crops in winter if you can't maintain the heat. This also gets expensive, and while your lighting will offset the heating, it can also become too much. Many newer grow lights use different technologies to get as hot as traditional grow lights, but they can still get toasty. If your lights get too hot, they can also become a fire hazard.

Hydroponic Grow Designs

Any hydroponic system must cover these five basic needs. Still, apart from this, your design does not need to have anything in common. There are thousands of ways of organizing your system, but there are three main types of course – NFT, Media Based, and Flood and Drain. These all include nutrient water running over the roots of plants using pumps; it's merely the arrangement and components that differ. There are also designs using a wick, water culture, and aeroponics.

NFT – Nutrient Film Technique

This is by far the most common growing technique you'll encounter in hydroponics and in aquaculture because it's easy to scale up and cheaper than the rest. Plants grow using gutters or growing towers where a thin layer of water runs through or across the roots. You can actually use NFT as part of your setup and use another design as the central arrangement depending on your available space. NFT is ideal for smaller rooms because it can be done as vertical towers instead of gutters. Tall or large plants aren't suited for NFT because the root area is too large to fit into the gutter or tower and still support the plant. It also means their roots won't get enough water causing them to die quickly or fail to grow to their potential.

The design uses less water than any other because there's practically nowhere for evaporation to occur except where the plant sits into the water. You can also design this system without a pump if it's tiny where you have the water tank higher lower than the grow bed and use gravity to push water out of the tank and then back up into it. Since it's impossible to regulate, this isn't ideal, but a small test design could be feasible. The reason it's better to have a pump doing this job is that you can guarantee the amount of nutrient solution flooding over your plants either at a constant or flooding rate. You know your water won't stagnate.

Media Based

Media beds are great for the average household system because they can get quite large, but they're the easiest to get into and see how things work. It uses a similar concept to NFT in that water flows in a layer over the plant roots, but since the beds can be quite deep, it's most suited for more extensive or tall plants.

You can also combine NFT towers or gutters with grow beds as long as your pump is strong enough.

It uses slightly more water than the NFT because the entire media bad allows for evaporation; this also means it's easier for the roots to get dry if your water level becomes low. It has a constant flow of water like the NFT to help get around this. This arrangement requires most media because you're using beds to get around this if you have smaller plants by using baskets.

Media beds are cumbersome and usually require more support than any other type. They're less suited for growing outside because of the evaporation rate and use the most space because of the bed and the amount of water. You'll need to make sure your foundations are correctly supported for safety. Another downside to this is that constant submersion roots can become rotted or fail to get enough oxygen.

Flood and Drain

The flood system is actually a derivative of the Media design. It uses smaller media beds or baskets and only floods them periodically. It's actually the most common design for beginners to start with and for school systems. It's handy and while it needs more space than an NFT arrangement, it's more flexible with the type of plants because there's less chance of the roots becoming rotten from being submerged. This system requires a pump and a timer so that you can set the amount and duration of the flood. Not all media is suited for the flood design because some float, which means your media will rise and fall with the water level and disturb the roots.

The most common type of small beginner system uses a bell siphon and water reservoir tank. This allows the water to flood and flow without the need for an electric pump. It's not very useful, significantly if water levels drop. If there's too much water, the siphon will simply flood continuously. This can cause the same problems as the media-based designs where the roots rot and become waterlogged.

Wick

A wicking system only works well for minimal arrangements. It's a simple reservoir and media bed design that uses an air pump and into the water reservoir to stop it stagnating and coconut, cotton, or another porous roping to soak up the water from the pool and into the media bed. It does not flood and only provides a minimum amount of water, but it's the most straightforward system. It does not need a big pump to circulate the water. There's also a lot of chance for evaporation.

Water Culture

A water culture system is ideal for small or large arrangements. It uses a floating raft (usually Styrofoam) to float the plants suspended directly into the water. It's the simplest of all since there's no need for a pump or pipes, but it's a good idea to have an air pump to keep the water from stagnating. This is ideal for lettuce and water-loving plants because there's no way the roots will dry out, and it prevents evaporation by limiting the surface exposed to air. However, there's a risk that the plant roots will rot because of being always submerged. It can easily be made out of an old aquarium for a desktop design for teaching. This isn't good for large plants or long-term growth because of the high chance of rot.

Aeroponics

An aeroponic system is by far the most complicated and technical. It uses a similar concept to NFT. Only a small nutrient system reaches the roots continually; only the plants are suspended in the air. The solution is applied as a constant mist.

The misting is usually cycled every few minutes to allow the roots exposed to air on a timer. This requires a much shorter timer than a flood system but allows for more evaporation and uses more water because it's constant. The design also tends to take up more space, and unless you have the entire thing enclosed will mean that there's a lot of excess spray outside of the root area, which can affect your electronics.

Chapter 1: Hydroponics for Beginners

The primary thing about hydroponics that anybody will see is that there is no requirement for soil. Plants just need soil for outdoor growing and gardening as the plant roots would develop and gather nutrients in the ground. Be that as it may, on the off chance that the soil is nutritionally lacking is nutrients, at that point, the plant would pass on. Hydroponics permits you to have authority over not just the kind of nutrient finding a good pace. Yet, the amount of the nutrient the plant would get.

With plant growth in soil, a ton of water is squandered through with hydroponics, the water is reused, and the nutrient admission of the plant is controlled. Typically, the plant specialist doesn't have to reestablish the nutrients for a little while in the water. With the water being reused and the nutrients being in the water, this keeps up a steady progression of nutrients to the plants.

There are many manners by which to convey the nutrients to the plants in hydroponics. The static solution can be offered straightforwardly to the foundations of the plant you are growing through a water-rich with nutrients in a compartment. The roots would essentially sit in the circulated air through the water while the blend would be continually washing over the underlying foundations of the plant; Things, for example, lettuce would utilize this sort of system as would potatoes. They would be that as it may be consistently washed over with moving water. This is generally used just in more significant hydroponic regions and ranches and not so much something utilized in-home hydroponics.

In aeroponics (which is a plant growing from off the ground, for example, plants hanging up), the underlying balancing foundations of the plants are splashed with a fog containing nutrients reasonable for plant growth. The water is in a similar compartment as the plants, yet the roots are not in the solution as they can develop farther than the holder. The seeds should be moistened to remain wet and took care of in a nutrient-rich condition.

The beneficial thing about hydroponic nurseries is that they just so happen to occupy significantly less room than regular cultivating and can be situated in your home or a toilet only as industrial facilities and even in general stores. They utilize less water, as referenced before, than soil plants as you control where the water goes, dissimilar to the soil that would simply absorb everything.

You find that you keep ailments from finding a workable pace that would, as a rule, happen outside because there are no pesticides and no extraordinary climate conditions. As you control the nutrients, you know what is going into your plants, so on the off chance that anything happens, you know precisely how to fix it. With outside growing, you can't generally forestall climate and soil conceived bugs. At the same time, inside, they are, for all intents and purposes, nonexistent.

Beginning with hydroponics can be a befuddling game. It is ideal to inquire about products and read help directs to completely comprehend what you are doing. You should search for suitable hydroponic hardware and hydroponic lighting and make sense of what you need to purchase directly for you, good karma growing with hydroponics.

1.1 Beginner's Guide On How To Make A Hydroponic System

A hydroponic system is a very complex setup, and there is much information that needs to be learned about it. The process of understanding how to make a hydroponic system work is one in which there are lots of steps involved, so the person creating it has to become really patient. However, if you want to build a system from scratch, you can also buy a system like a HydroHut Deluxe, and then all the figuring out has been done for you.

Step By Step

One of the very first and most essential points anyone understanding how to make a hydroponic system needs to learn is that the actual layout of the system is actually only going to be restricted by the desires of the designer. In other words, you can genuinely go full-scale and build whichever sort of hydroponic structure that you want.

An additional step in understanding how to make a hydroponic system is to gather the required components. These will certainly vary according to what the creator wants the system to look like. Still, one of the most standard and essential items is a standard tray. Remember that the system should provide means both to support the plant and to aerate the system. A person can create a more complex system with much more expensive materials, but then at the same time, they can also buy it for almost the same price.

An essential tip to remember when understanding how to make a hydroponic system is that short plants, for example, lettuce and spinach, will probably support themselves. These are indeed the best options to go with since they will have less threat of suffering from complications. Additionally, take into account that you will find some great hydroponic grow tents offered that one can purchase and which will probably be of great help.

You will also find a lot of great resources available that are going to be useful to any person trying to learn how to make a hydroponic system, in particular those on the Internet. This is since, with the web, an individual can browse through literally hundreds of various websites in a matter of minutes, something that obviously could not be done otherwise. The best thing to do here would be to go on a search engine on the World Wide Web and type in "hydroponic grow tent," and then the diverse available options will pop up. The most essential thing to bear in mind is that the most simple and effective system is a Hydro Hut.

1.2 A Beginners Guide To Hydroponics And Organic Hydroponic Gardening

Hydroponics, simply depicted, is a method of growing plants using water blended nourishment solutions. Soil isn't utilized in the growing procedure by any stretch of the imagination, which settles on it a mainstream decision for gardening. It involves more effectiveness and a decreased danger of pesticides and other plant borne diseases. Going above and beyond, individuals have begun utilizing organic hydroponic gardening to develop palatable things like fruits and vegetables.

This may come as a shock to the individuals who had never connected organic plant cultivation with hydroponics; however, looking at the situation objectively, the principle ingredients utilized in hydroponics are either virtually organic in nature (water) or can be made organic (the nutrients and compost). So it is entirely conceivable to seek after organic hydroponic gardening.

Increasingly About Hydroponics

The word Hydroponics originates from the Greek language (hydro importance water and ponos significance work). As referenced above, it is a method for developing plants, utilizing water blended in with nutrients and growing media, such as perlite, rock, and mineral fleece. No soil is required since soil just goes about as a nutrient store. It gets the job done, along these lines, to supply the nutrient solution to the plant roots misleadingly.

Hydroponics has demonstrated to be a fascinating improvement in the territory of indoor gardening. The fundamental reasons why plant producers have embraced hydroponics relate, for the most part, to cost-effectiveness and proficiency. The

1.3 Advantages Of Hydroponics Include:

- No soil is required
- there is steady and considerable plant yield
- The danger of pests and diseases is extensively diminished
- The expense of water is altogether lower since, as a rule, the water can be reused There is less space, growing time, and work included

- The expense of nourishment likewise demonstrates to beneath, since the nutrients blended in with water are recyclable

- There is, for all intents and purposes, no nourishment pollution inferable from the way that hydroponics is a controlled method of plant cultivation and can be worked in a shielded territory, utilizing artificial lighting.

To abridge, the fame of hydroponics can be credited to a higher pace of plant growth, just as the way that since it doesn't include the utilization of soil, it tends to be utilized to develop plants in places where generally it is beyond the realm of imagination to expect to lead in-ground horticultural or gardening exercises.

1.4 What Is Organic Hydroponic Gardening

The word organic is utilized to depict whatever exudes from the earth, similar to plants, creatures, and vegetables. Organic Gardening, in this way, infers no misleadingly evolved ingredients are utilized in the plant cultivation process. All things considered, one of the principal elements in hydroponics, water, is organic. Organic compost can likewise be gotten from cows, chicken, kelp, sheep fertilizer, bones, and other a few other natural sources.

It might be important here that alongside the water blended nutrients, plants additionally require air and nitrogen to develop and flourish well. Moreover, there likewise needs a sufficient substance of pH (potential Hydrogen) in the manure. Hydroponics led with an organic compost alongside other organic gardening forms brings about more extravagant, better plant yields.

An eminent bit of leeway of organic hydroponics is determining the consolidated outcomes that originate from soil-based hydroponic gardening. This assists with getting rid of making the best mix of synthetic concoctions, which, if customarily not done, prompts plant crumbling.

1.5 Plant Transplantation

The uplifting news about hydroponic and organic hydroponic gardening is that you transfer your plants developed with soil to a hydroponic system. This simply involves delicately separating the plants from the soil and running its underlying foundations under some virus water. At long last, you can put the roots into your hydroponic pot or holder and spread it with your growing media.

In conclusion, it is sheltered to state that hydroponic and organic hydroponic gardening makes it conceivable to accomplish cleaner and more beneficial environmental conditions. Lastly, individuals who have utilized these methods of plant cultivation have seen it as hugely fun and beneficial. In this way, why pause? Feel free to start your hydroponics garden today!

1.6 Usable Lighting Types

Lighting plays a crucial role in plant growth, and therefore will be an essential part of your hydroponic growth system. Through photosynthesis, plants convert light - which is from the sun in nature - into sugars that energize a plant's growth. This is a result of chlorophyll located in the leaf cells that uses light and combines this with carbon dioxide and water - the end result is sugar and oxygen that is metabolized and transformed into energy for growth.

This makes the quality of the light you use vital for the prosperity of your plants. What we must aim to do within our hydroponic setup is to emulate the morning that the sun produces with an artificial light source. Let's explore how you can best achieve this to guarantee positive results.

Natural lights

One of the most important things you need to learn about when you are learning about growing with hydroponics, besides the existing system, is the lighting.

If your plants do not receive the light they need, they are not going to grow correctly, nor are they going to produce the amount of fruit you want. To become the best grower, you always want to find out what is limiting you the most. Learning what is modifying you the most and learning as much about it as you can allow you to increase the growth of your plants without adjusting anything else.

When you think about lighting, you have to realize that no matter how great your system is, no matter how great the medium you are using is, no matter how high the quality of your fertilizer, without the proper light, your plants will never be able to grow healthy, vigorous plants.

The first thing you have to know about is the color of light that your bulbs produce. You see, every bulb will produce a colored light that is measured in degrees Kelvin; this is how the hue produced by the bulb is specified.

Most plants are going to grow better with a bulb that is 6500° degrees, Kelvin. Flowering plants, on the other hand, are going to grow better at 2700k degrees Kelvin.

Of course, many different variables will affect the rate at which your plants grow. Still, the most important of these variables is light. Using a high-quality light is the only way you can guarantee your plants will grow to their fullest potential.

Artificial lights

There are several lighting systems on the market today. Each of these systems has its own pros and cons that need to be taken into consideration. Still, you need to remember that choosing the correct lighting for your indoor growing is the most important thing you can do to ensure significant growth.

Incandescent lamps are the first of the lighting systems that I want to talk about. These are what are known as the standard household light bulbs, and they are not very efficient when it comes to growing plants. They actually only have about a 5% efficiency rate. Incandescent lamps are not recommended for growing plants.

Fluorescent lights are a great choice if you are planning on growing your plants indoors. The best fluorescent lights are high output lights, which are about 7 times more efficient. This simply means that the lights will put out more light while using less electricity. A wide range of spectrums are available for fluorescent lamps, and the 6500k is the best for indoor growing.

If you are growing larger plants, fluorescent lighting is not advised as these are better for smaller plants. The fluorescent lamps are not as good at penetrating as the high-intensity discharge lamps are.

There are many options for growing plants when it comes to fluorescent lights. You can choose lights that will be hung above the plants or hung to the side of the plants.

Another prevalent form of fluorescent lights is the compact fluorescent lights or CFLs. These were designed as an alternative to regular household bulbs or incandescent lights because they use less electricity and are supposed to have a longer life than incandescent bulbs.

The CFL's are suitable for growers who are on a small budget and are growing small plants.

The great thing about CFLs is that you do not have to worry about the wiring, they don't require anything more than a standard socket, and they are extremely low in price. If you are going to use CFLs, you should consider using a reflector of some type; otherwise, you will be wasting a lot of light that you could be using for your plants.

 High-intensity discharge lamps are the next type of lighting that I want to talk to you about. Also known as HID, these bulbs are the top pick for most growers. These are usually the types that are generally used in street lights, parking lots, and warehouses. These lights are the top pick for today's growers because their output is 8 times more efficient than regular household light bulbs.

Light-emitting diodes or LEDs are some of the new technology that growers utilize for their plants because they use much less electricity than the other light sources mentioned.

There are many different things you need to think about when you are choosing your lighting. Your budget is the first thing that you need to think about when you are choosing your lighting for your hydroponics system. Those who are working with a low budget will be better off using T5 fluorescent tubes as will small scale growers.

If you have a large budget, the HID lamps are the highest quality. Still, you will need to consider getting them their own ventilation system because they will significantly raise the temperature of the room otherwise.

LED lights are great for those who will be growing for an extended period because they will save you a ton of money on your electric bill. For example, some growers save as much as $5,000 over the lifetime of their LED bulbs.

Of course, this is just an example. It all depends on the price of electricity, how much you are willing to invest upfront, how often you use the lights, the type of environment the lighting system will be in, and so forth.

Once you have chosen your hydroponics system and your medium, you will need to spend some time thinking about the type of lighting system you will be using. It is important to remember that the lighting system is the most crucial factor in growing your plants indoors. It is not something you should take lightly.

Chapter 2: Build Your Own Hydroponic System

Plan many relatively simple hydroponic systems that are pictured below. When building your own system, keep in mind: always get all the parts and materials before starting. Otherwise, you may find that you have drilled a specific diameter of the drainage pipe, and you cannot find the right size plug to match it. Consult Resource Lists for items like pumps, clocks, and tubing, as well as other resources associated with hydroponics.

2.1 Deep-water Culture

To create your DWC hydroponics system, you'll need the following:

- Five-gallon bucket
- Air pump
- Airstone
- Airline tubing
- Net pots
- Growing medium of choice
- Hydroponic nutrients (to put in the water)

You can get all of these supplies for under $100. Compare this to traditional soil gardening, where you need—depending upon your exact gardening conditions, of course—a lawnmower, a hand trowel, a rake, a shovel, gardening gloves, a hose, a rain barrel, bags of soil and mulch, and fertilizer, and will potentially have to pay for landscaping, as well.

All of those can run up into thousands of dollars in pricing, and that's if you even have the room for a proper soil garden in the first place. Even if you're growing on your balcony, you need most gardening tools, gloves, hose or watering can, pots, and so on.

The method of setting up your DWC is simple: you fill the bucket with water, then fill that with the proper amount of pH and nutrients. Then you connect the air tubing, the air stone, and the air pump, placing the air stone in the bucket. You then place the seeds in the growing material in the net pots, which you place floating on top of the water.

This is a popular method because of how easy it is. The plants grow quickly—you can harvest lettuce in 30 days with this method. In contrast, in the soil, it takes lettuce twice as long to be harvested. Just make sure your plants are getting enough air, or the roots will drown.

As you get more experience with this, if you want to grow different kinds of plants, you can set up other plants in different buckets, and then cut holes in each bucket, one on each side, and feed a tube to connect each bucket together. The water flows from the reservoir and then is pumped into each bucket in turn, eventually circling back to the pool.

This is for when you get more experience, however, and depends on if you have the room for such an operation. But if you do have space and want to do it, it's a hands-free method that allows you to grow tons of plants.

2.2 Nutrient Film Technique (NFT)

This is a great system to use, straightforward maintenance—not, however, for plants with deep root systems. Plants with deep roots can clog up the channels, so you'll want to use something like a DWC for those plants.

To set up an NFT system, you need:

- A reservoir (can be a solid bucket or plastic tote)
- Air pump
- Airstone
- Airline tubing
- Water pump
- Net pots
- Growing medium
- Hydroponic nutrients
- NFT channels

An NFT system of channels is a place to house your plants and growing media. However, if you're doing this at home, there's an easy way to make your own NFT channels: PVC pipes. Just cut holes in them that are big enough for you to put your net pots and plants in, and you're good to go.

Another option is to use rain gutters, or a 2x4 that you've lined with plastic sheeting. These aren't round, like a PVC pipe, so you'll be sure to hit all of the roots evenly with your water solution. With PVC pipe, you have to be more careful in your setup to not accidentally end up missing some roots and drying them out.

Set up the reservoir just like you would for the DWC system but set the plant-filled PVC pipes or rain gutters up on a slight angle or slope so that the water naturally runs down the channel and back into the reservoir.

Remember that the plants closest to the source of the water will get the most and best nutrients, so don't have channels that are too long—keep them short and have multiple channels rather than one long one.

You can also rotate plants while they're still small or take the tube out of one end and reverse the direction of the flow every couple of weeks to keep the growth of plants even.

Again, you can get most of these supplies for under $100. The PVC pipes, rain gutters, or proper NFT channels if you really want them, will cost a bit more.

You'll want to check up on your roots every so often to make sure that they're okay. Roots should be bright white and flourishing.

2.3 Aeroponics

This is a system that you should probably buy from a company. You can set it up yourself, but it's easier and generally less expensive to buy the pre-packaged version and use this exclusively for herbs. The herbs don't take up a lot of room, and you can keep the system on a kitchen counter, the side of a desk, an end table, or so on.

It will also free up space in any other hydroponics system to grow food and plants if you so desire, so you don't have to worry about your tomatoes or peonies overcrowding your thyme and basil. There are plenty of great options out there, but if you just go to your local garden store, they can recommend one for you that's inexpensive and will give you the results you need.

2.4 Wicking

This is another simple and easy method to use. And, depending upon how much control you want and if you're growing many different kinds of plants, you can do a wicking system in just a two-liter bottle.

For a bottle, you just cut the bottle in half, then turn the top half upside down and place it in the bottom half after you fill the bottom half with the water solution. You then put a cotton rope through the opening, fill the top half with your growing medium, and plant your plant. Viola!

On a larger scale, you'll need:

- Growing medium that's conducive to wicking, such as perlite
- Reservoir container
- Wick material like rope, string, or felt
- Container for the plants so they're held in place
- Airstone

Simply fill the reservoir with your water and solutions, put the airstone in the water, and then take your plant container and poke holes in it for the wick to be fed through. Measure carefully so that you don't make holes that are too big and lead to leaking.

Feed the wicks into the container, fill with the growing medium, and then plant your plants in the growing medium and watch them grow!

It's best to do this with the two-liter bottle method if you have an odd living space or don't have a lot of room. You have one plant per bottle, and you can set them anywhere you like. This will also support larger plants such as vegetables and fruits.

2.5 Drip

The drip method is beneficial if you've got a lot of room, and you want to grow a lot of plants. Otherwise, it can be a bit of overkill. But if you've got that and you want that, there's no better system.

This is fantastic if you have a small greenhouse — it won't need to be larger than, say, 8 x 12 feet — because you can grow enough to feed your entire family, or even to sell, in that small space. But that's if you want to get really fancy with it. To create your basic, easy-to-use drip system, here's how.

You will need:

- Four five-gallon buckets
- Four through holes (also known as bulkhead fittings)
- Black vinyl tubing
- Submersible fountain pump
- 18- to 30-gallon reservoir
- Growing medium
- Furnace filter so growing medium doesn't get into the tubing
- Your nutrients and pH balancers
- Connecting "T" for the tubing

All of this, again, you can get for about $100, and except for the nutrients, you can get the supplies at any local hardware store. The most expensive item will probably be the fountain pump, which tends to go around $40.

First, drill holes in the buckets for the through holes/bulkhead fittings to go into. Be sure to measure carefully, so there aren't any leaks.

You'll also want to spray paint these buckets, usually with black paint, so that light can't get in them and cause algae to grow. Only paint the outside so that no paint will get on the plants inside.

Fill the first third of your bucket with rocks to weigh it down and help with drainage. Be sure to rinse, bleach, and then rinse the rocks before putting them in the bucket so that no soil diseases get transferred to the plants via the rocks.

Place your growing medium on top of the rocks. Place your plant in the growing material, and then create a circle with the tubing, connecting it with the "T." Do this with all four buckets. Once that's done, you'll want to take a paperclip and heat one end with a candle, then use this to punch some holes in the tubing ring. You'll also probably want to cut a notch in the top of the bucket to hold the tubing securely.

You then connect the tubing to the bulkhead fitting and then lead that tubing back to the reservoir. So, the tubing goes up from the pool, through to the buckets where it "drips" out the holes in the tubing, drains down through the rocks, and goes back down into the reservoir.

Ta-da! It takes a bit more work to set up than other systems, but it's great for gardening more plants and is inexpensive and can be done in one afternoon.

2.6 Ebb and Flow

Finally, we have an ebb and flow system. It's not relatively as low maintenance as the DWC system. However, it's still one of the lowest maintenance systems and is easy to set up and use if you have multiple plants you want to grow. You also have a wider surface area to grow your plants without enlarging your reservoir, which is the trouble you can run into with DWC. It's also easier to control the temperature of your solution when the pool isn't in the same container as the plants.

You will need:

- Container for the plants to grow in

- Pool

- Submersible fountain pump

- A timer to turn the pump on and off

- Tubing to run the water up from the reservoir into the plant container

- An overflow tube set to the height you want the water level

- Growing medium and nutrients supplies

- Net pots

Set up your plant container—a square or rectangular tray—and set it on top of a table, with the reservoir underneath. Fill your pool with water and the nutrient solution, put in the fountain pump, and connect it to the timer. Then set up the tubing to run up into the tray and then an overflow tube to run back down into the reservoir.

The downside to this is that you'll want to fill the entire tray with an easily-draining growing medium, which uses a lot more growing medium than other systems. You'll also need to check for algae regularly and make sure that it doesn't grow because of the light and nutrients. Make sure that your reservoir is covered and dark and that you check your growing solution.

As with the other systems, this shouldn't cost you more than $100 or so, and voila, you have your own system for growing plants. Some people combine different techniques, such as starting their plants in an ebb and flow and then transferring them to a DWC or an NFT. It's all based on your needs and most comfortable for you. Still, all of these methods are inexpensive, easy to set up, easy to maintain and keep in your home, and yield results.

Chapter 3: How to Maintain a Hydroponic System

3.1 How to Make the System Stable

Hydroponic gardens need to have proper care and maintenance, or they will not produce healthy plants. Not only do they need to be cleaned continuously, but various maintenance checks need to be carried out to make sure the system remains functioning correctly.

A faulty drain or a leaky pipe or switch could do severe damage to a hydroponic garden as most of the systems rely on their equipment and parts to work smoothly.

Cleanliness

To stop the build-up of algae, mold, and fungus or stop attracting pests, keep the growing room as clean as possible. Equipment should be flushed and cleaned at least twice a month to maintain water levels, prevent algae growth, and ensure that no pests are lurking about the system.

To stop pests and various fungal growth, growers should always make sure their hands are clean. Hands should be kept washed, especially after handling anything that was dirty or in contact with a harmful substance.

Do not let old fallen leaves, stems, fruit, produce, or growing media or even pots or discarded trays lie around the growing areas. Rather throw out any debris or broken items, and wash and pack away any unused equipment.

Wash all equipment after use and only reuse a growing medium if it can be reused, and it has been thoroughly washed and sterilized. In fact, all growing mediums, whether old or new, should be thoroughly cleaned before being used as not to contaminate the grow pots, grow trays, and the reservoir.

Keeping the growing area and equipment clean cuts down on the chances of infestation and development of frustrating diseases that are a nuisance to get rid of.

Nutrient solution

The proper nutrient solution for the plant type and system type should be used at the correct ratio of solution to water.

Only use good quality nutrient solutions with an organic base. Advance nutrients are only required should there be a problem that needs to be fixed, such as a nutrient deficiency in a plant.

The nutrient solution balance should be checked regularly especially is it is a recovery system where the solution is being continuously recycled.

Ensure that the solution is flushed and wholly refreshed regularly. There is no salt buildup since this is very acidic and toxic to the plants.

Watering

Watering is done in many different ways and is delivered to each of the hydroponic systems differently.

Make sure the water is always fresh and checked regularly. Algae is a common problem, as is nutrient build up in the system. An oxygen pump should be installed to ensure the water is being well hydrated and to keep the water fresher for longer.

Water solutions can come from the tap, drain systems, or rain collection tanks.

Watering can be on a continuous flow basis or set by a timer that switches on and off at different intervals during the day.

If possible, a person should always have a backup water solution available if an emergency and their primary watering source is unavailable. Some plants are susceptible to their watering schedule, and even a few minute's downtimes and a missed watering schedule can cause some damage.

Reservoir temperature

The water in the reservoir should be around 65 to 75 degrees Fahrenheit, a basic room temperature. Water that is either too hot or too cold can damage the plant's root systems and leaves.

The reservoir should be topped off with water to keep pH and nutrient levels constant. Change out the water regularly.

Humidity

Different plants and hydroponic systems need the humidity to be on different levels. Some thermometers can measure the moisture and temperature to ensure that the plants are comfortable. Keeping an optimum level does not encourage the growth of unwanted diseases and fungi.

Make sure plants that love the hotter temperatures get enough humidity by giving them a regular misting spray. This will help to keep the moisture constant for the plants that do not like too much humid.

3.2 Inspect the equipment

The equipment should be thoroughly inspected regularly.

Many things can go wrong in a hydroponic system, especially with the equipment.

And the best way to troubleshoot is to try to avoid as many equipment malfunctions as possible.

The best way to inspect equipment is to keep the entire system in mind. When doing the inspection, start at one point and work your way through your system.

Start with the reservoir and all the systems that are dependent on it.

Water feeding pipe

This should be thoroughly checked for crimps that may not be feeding the solution correctly.

Nutrients build up in the pipes, so they may need thorough flushing out or replacing.

Check for any blockages in the pipe.

Check for any holes or leaks that could deter the flow of water pressure in the pipe.

Check for any algae or mold that may be growing in or around the pipe.

Determine if it may be time to replace the hoses.

Give them a good cleaning if they are still viable.

Nozzles and hoses

Check the nozzles that feed the root systems, sprinklers, or misting systems.

When last were they changed?

Check for blockages or leakage.

Check any joins and washers for leaks.

Check for sediment build-up, algae, or mold growing in or around these attachments.

Give them a good cleaning if they are still usable.

Drain siphons and hoses

Check the drain pipes for blockages

When last were they replaced?

Check for leaks.

Check for algae or mold growing in or around these pipes.

They may need to have a good cleaning as part of the system maintenance.

Check the reservoir water pump

Test the pump

Make sure it is still working correctly and pumping the water at the optimum flow.

Check that all pump attachments are not leaking air.

Check the reservoir

Check that there is no build-up, algae, or mold growing in the reservoir.

Check for any leaks.

Make sure the water is at the optimum temperature for the hydroponic system and plants.

Check that any air pumps are functioning correctly and adequately oxygenating the tank.

Make sure any oxygen stones do not have unwanted algae or mold growth on them

Growing trays

Make sure the growing tray(s) do not have any leaks in them.

Make sure the growing tray(s) are clean and have not unwanted algae or mold growing on them.

Clean off any nutrient build-up and make sure the trays are clean.

For a closed system, the trays must be given thorough flushing out.

Growing pots

Check that each of the pots is still intact and not broken.

Replace any that are not functioning correctly.

Ensure any growing medium is clean and does not have any unwanted algae or mold growing on them that could upset the plant's natural balance.

Lighting equipment

Check that the bulbs are still functioning correctly.

Check that the lighting is still adequate for the environment.

Check the timers are working correctly.

Clean any residue off the lighting system.

Temperature

Make sure that any thermostat is working correctly and that room temperature is average.

Check that the humidity is correct for the growing environment.

Check both the temperature and humidity thermometers to ensure that they are still working correctly.

Ventilation

Make sure that there is adequate ventilation in the growing room.

Not enough ventilation can cause mold.

Check that all fans and cooling systems are working correctly.

Support Systems

Check that any hanging supports for the plants are working without causing the plant or system any undue stress.

Make sure that the environment in which the hydroponic system is housed offers the correct infrastructure for the system to function correctly.

Make sure the plants are all supported and planted correctly to ensure a successful infrastructure.

Tools

Are all the gardening tools in working order?

Are they cleaned?

Are there any that may need to be replaced?

3.3 Look At Your Plants

Make sure you keep a vigilant check on your growing plants. Measure their growth rate, root growth, and when they are ready to harvest.

This gives a person a good measure of how the next batch should perform and something to determine if the growing medium, solution, or systems structure may need to be changed or optimized.

The plants must also be checked to ensure they are getting enough nutrients, they are growing as they should, and there are no pests or other infestations. A lot of growing problems and deficiencies can be caused by various infestations. Some are easy to spot, others may take more of an experienced eye, but as a gardener gets to know their plants, they will come to instinctively know when something is wrong.

Look for the signs in seedlings such as slow growth, looking sad and droopy, white fluffy stuff growing on the leaves, etc.

Take the time to look over the plants; do not just rush through it. If there are a lot of plants to look over, break them into sections and do a revolving sweep of one section on this day, and the next section on another.

If there is an outbreak, you will need to go through the entire growing area right away.

Spending time with the plants in a hydroponic environment can also be quite useful for the mind and spirit. Plants and running water are somewhat therapeutic and can reduce stress, anxiety, and ease tension.

3.4 Change One Thing At A Time

If you want to change or expand your system, do not try and do it all at once.

Choose a section to change, switch it around, or upgrade and start with that.

Before rushing out and buying expensive parts, why not try a bit of DIY and try to make it yourself. Or at least look around to see what you have available before rushing off to spend more money on an item you do not really need.

Hydroponic systems are not only flexible and versatile in what they can grow or how they deliver their solutions, but they can also be easily adapted to suit the grower's needs and lifestyle.

There are so many great DIY ideas on creating the perfect hydroponic garden online these days that it is well worth a try. The money you save building the system yourself can be better spent on plants, growing media, or nutrient solutions.

To keep a system simple and working for you, think carefully about an upgrade or addition. Plot it out and then work through one section to get that part right before moving on to the next.

Chapter 4: Maintenance of Your Garden

One of the key ingredients to being successful with hydroponic gardening is preparing to spend the time necessary to maintain your garden and your plants. I cannot stress how important it is to continue to monitor your garden, to make sure that it is running correctly and that your plants are actually growing and thriving.

Some maintenance is necessary daily, some weekly, and some less frequently. We will cover the six most important factors that must be considered to ensure that your system is functioning correctly and if there are problems, how to identify them, and overcome them as quickly as possible. Your garden is an investment, and you need to make sure that your investment is protected. The main aim when it comes to maintenance of a system failure is recovery.

Some systems need very little to no maintenance at all. Still, for the purpose of understanding and gaining some additional knowledge and information, we will look at systems that need to be looked after regularly. A well-maintained garden will be a garden that can run with as little maintenance and attention as possible. A top tip for maintaining your garden would be to monitor it regularly, making it easier to pick up problems as quickly as possible. You would want to do this to resolve them without putting your plants at risk or in danger.

We will look at all of the critical ingredients that make for the smooth running of your hydroponic system, namely: air, water, the correct temperature for your plan, pH balance, controls, and finally, overall plant care.

4.1 Aeration

The first of these areas that we need to look at when it comes to maintenance is aeration, or in other words, how much air or oxygen is necessary for your plants to grow and grow well.

All living cells that are found in plants need oxygen to be able to convert sugar into energy. While this oxygen is naturally created during photosynthesis, it usually only means that the leaves can get this oxygen. Plants that are grown within soil have to work harder to find this oxygen. When they have possibly been overwatered, or been in an environment where there has been flooding, they can often be referred to as drowning. The main reason for using this term is because the root structure of the plant (which has also needed oxygen) has been deprived of the oxygen that it desperately needs, and the entire plant will die. This is one of the main reasons why the nutrient solution and the substrate or growing medium is so important when it comes to your hydroponic garden. You need to make sure that your plant receives the right amount of oxygen or aeration via the root system.

Oxygen is needed around the root structure because this is the environment that the nutrients that you have mixed in your nutrient-rich solution above need to survive. Remember that the nutrient solution is what contains all your beneficial microorganisms and will allow for these to be absorbed through the root system.

In your system, it is essential to know how your substrates will act or react to aeration, and this will give you a better understanding of which substrate you should use to produce the best possible result when it comes to maintaining your garden and making sure that the roots of each of your plants receive the correct amount of oxygen that they need to grow and thrive.

In your hydroponic system, a large portion of the oxygen that the plant needs will be absorbed from the air. A large proportion of this oxygen will also be dissolved in the water-based solution that contains the nutrients. Some examples of how hydroponic systems effectively provide aeration to the root structures of plants are typically in the ebb and flow or flood and drain system. Here, the oxygen is absorbed by the roots as the nutrient solution drains away into the holding reservoir.

Another way of looking at how this whole system works with dissolved oxygen being found in the nutrient solution would be to think of these molecules as having a slightly different structure to the average water molecule ($H20$) but being one that can be absorbed by the roots of the plants instead. This is a crucial element in keeping the roots of your plants aerated. There must be enough dissolved oxygen available in the nutrient solution.

Two things will affect these oxygen levels. The first is the level of dissolved inorganic salt found in the water (also referred to as salinity), and the second is temperature. Salinity will be easily recognized as being a problem a lot quicker than being able to pick up that there is a problem with dissolved oxygen. Salinity will show up as toxic shock. On the other hand, temperature plays a vital role in how the solution can retain dissolved oxygen. The higher the temperature, the less likely it can hold the dissolved oxygen. Ideal temperatures should be between 65-72 degrees F. Fluctuations between below these temperatures will result in plants growing a lot slower than they should do. At the same time, anything above this will reduce the ability of the solution to retain the dissolved oxygen.

Controlling the temperature of the nutrient solution can be done in a couple of ways – the pool that holds the nutrient solution can simply be removed from where the growing space is (in a warmer environment), submersible heating systems (similar to the ones used in fish tanks or aquariums) can be used if the water temperature is too cold. If the water is too warm, you could also look at using a chilling water system.

When the dissolved oxygen has been absorbed by the root system it needs to be replaced. The easiest way of doing this is by using air stones and an air pump to pump air into the nutrient solution directly. The bubbles disrupt the surface of the solution and inject air directly into the nutrients. If the temperature within the nutrient solution reservoir is within the range we mentioned above, dissolved oxygen can be replenished without any problems.

Another way of replacing the depleted oxygen in the nutrient solution is by using hydrogen peroxide (H_2O_2). The molecular structure of hydrogen peroxide is actually water, with another unstable oxygen molecule. There is quite a debate as to whether this is effective or not. Most hydroponic professionals believe that it can be beneficial if it is used in moderation and diluted thoroughly. One of the main reasons why people think that it can be helpful to your system is that it is commonly found in rainwater. A downside of using this, though, would be that if it is too strong (has not been diluted sufficiently), it can damage those microorganisms that are necessary for the plant to grow.

Oxygen needs to be carried to the bottom of the root structure. When the levels of oxygen are kept constant, the plant can stay healthy, and growth can be stimulated.

When you keep your root system aerated sufficiently, this prevents the roots from drowning, and ultimately dying because they are being starved of the oxygen that they need. It is important to monitor this almost daily to make sure that your system is running. Ensure your nutrient reservoir's air pump and airstone system are working well enough so that the roots are getting all the oxygen that then need.

The next key ingredient to growing your garden with success is managing your water system.

4.2 Water

It is widely believed that you should be changing your water in your hydroponics system on average every two to three weeks. However, the deciding factor for this would really be the type of system that you are using. The main aim of water in your system is that you maintain your pH and nutrient levels. While changing your water is essential, the way that you change it is just as important.

Under normal conditions, your nutrient reservoir or regular water reservoir system is very likely to lose specific amounts of water due to natural evaporation and the uptake of this into the plants. To give you a better understanding of this, if you have a setup that is in direct sunlight or under artificial lights to stimulate growth and your climate is warmer, you are more likely to experience higher levels of evaporation than if you were in colder weather, and your plants were indoors, without being stimulated by lights.

Some other factors that can have a direct and negative impact on evaporation are if you have no cover over your reservoir at all. The number of plants that you have and how closely they are positioned to one another will also affect how much water you use and lose.

What this really means is that if you are growing a leafy green vegetable such as butter lettuce etc. you will need to add water more often than when you are growing plants in a colder climate. When you have a system with smaller water reservoirs, these will also need to be topped up with fresh water more often than larger ones.

Much of this is trial and error and paying close attention to what your water levels look like. If you see that there is a drastic water reduction, look at topping it up daily. If not, then this can be done every few days or maybe even weekly. A really great tip would be to establish a routine once you become more comfortable with your system – that way, you will know exactly how much water needs to be topped up. Something that you can do to help you with this routine is putting together a waterlog. Make a note of your water changes, how often, how much, and any specific pH (we will cover this in greater detail below). Following are two methods of dealing with your required water changes that I would recommend:

The first is topping up your water pool whenever you notice that the water will get lower. This is done with water that is pH neutral and clean. The most important part of this, apart from making sure that the water has the right pH spectrum and is free of contaminants, keeps an accurate record of how much water you are adding and more or less when. The reason for keeping these records is to identify once you have completed the replacement of more than half of the total volume of your reservoir capacity; at this stage, it is time for you to complete a much larger water change.

This is done by draining half of the water volume and replacing it with fresh water, for example – if your reservoir holds 50-gallons of water. You have changed out or topped up 25-gallons of water over a few weeks. It will now be time for you to empty out 25-gallons of water from the reservoir and replace it with another 25-gallons of clean, pH-balanced water). How often you need to make these changes will really depend on the size of the system that you are using.

Changing the water entirely on its own is never recommended. The main reason for this is because water can contain some harmful compounds that can kill off your plants. These compounds include things like ammonia or nitrates. However, if the water in your reservoir is allowed to stand, it can attract bacteria and fungi. Have you ever seen rainwater that has gathered in a container over time? That green and brown slimy substance at the bottom of the stagnant water is really harmful to your plants and can result in root rot. To prevent this, changing water should be done on a regular, consistent basis, where the pH is neutral, and the nutrient levels are also correct. If you remove half of the water, replacing it with half freshwater, it is reasonably easy to add only half of your nutrient solution that you would have started your system off with.

At the same time, it's essential to keep some of your "old" water in the system, because often there are beneficial bacteria that assist the uptake of nutrients in your system.

4.3 Temperature

Trying to find exactly the right temperature for your plants to grow optimally could take some work. The climate and temperature of your garden can have a direct influence on the quantity of your plant yield, as well as the quality of the crop itself. Climate would typically consist of humidity and temperature, and these two things can influence how the plant grows.

One of the most important things to consider when it comes to temperature is that it needs to remain as constant as possible. What this means is that the weather is the same all the time. This can be achieved by using grow lights, fans that can circulate the air from one part of the grow room or greenhouse to the next (this would really only be necessary for larger growing areas). The main benefit of using fans to circulate air is that plants prefer for the temperature to remain constant and consistent. Another solution could be a split air-conditioning unit. However, the costs of this are substantially more than what someone who is just starting out with this hobby would probably be prepared to spend.

Once again, depending on what you are growing, try, and find out what the ultimate temperature is that your plants need to thrive. These temperatures vary and so it is essential to make sure that you determine what temperature is best suited to all stages of the plant growth.

This is probably going to mean experimenting. When you are conducting these experiments, look at how the air temperature will affect the root structure of the plants. Remember that the higher the temperature in the growing environment, the higher the temperature is likely to be around the root structure.

If you live in colder climates and you need to increase the temperatures that are required by your plants, you can probably still achieve this by using a thermostat and a fan. This is worth mentioning for those who cannot afford all of the expensive air circulation or air conditioning equipment. Ideal temperatures for starting out with your hydroponic garden should range between 70°-80°F (21.1°-26.6°C).

If the temperature fluctuates drastically between the day and night, or when the lights are on and off, this is important to be able to recognize what the ideal temperature is for your plants to grow. Once this perfect temperature has been established, it becomes easier to regulate the optimal growing temperature. It is recommended that the variation between keeping the lights off and lights on temperature be kept within 10-15 degrees Fahrenheit to prevent mold and fungi, and other organisms that would typically threaten the plant.

Depending on the stage of the plant's growth, the required temperatures may vary. Temperatures needed for cloning and germinating or growing seedlings need to be consistent. For these plants, they need much warmer conditions. During this early root development, using small seedling heating mats may be an option. For the ideal germination temperatures, refer to the seed packets as these will give you all the technical data and information that you need.

Chapter 5: How to Choose a System

5.1 Choosing the Right Hydroponic System

What Are You Growing?

This is a major influencing decision because different plants are suited to different growing environments. If you are planning on growing a few vegetables, then a smaller system will do, but if you want to grow more, then you will need a more extensive system. If you are planning on growing plants that need different conditions, then you are likely going to need multiple systems or one where you can grow the plants in pots rather than in the same conditions as everything else. Considering what you will grow before you buy your hydroponic system is necessary to ensure the best outcomes from your hydroponic system. So, choose a plant that should meet your requirements. For example: if you have less space, then you can choose to grow some herbs or vegetables that generally need less space as compared to other plants. You can quickly grow some herbs or vegetables on your patio or balcony for family consumption. Flowering plants need a unique combination of nutrients, pH, and minerals, so use a bigger hydroponics system to hold enough of the single flower plants. If you want to grow hydroponics for a commercial purpose and you have ample space, then use different combinations of hydroponics that suit the plant you wish to cultivate.

Before you start shopping for your hydroponic system, you need to understand what you will grow and how much of it.

Will It Fit?

Considering the space that you are going to use for your hydroponics is another primary consideration. You must measure your distance to fit your hydroponics system properly. You should seek to use your space effectively so that your hydroponics get enough sunlight and air throughout the day for proper growth. This step becomes mandatory when you are using a patio or balcony for your hydroponics. Most systems come with the dimensions listed on them, but if you build hydroponics from scratch, then take a tank that should fit your space correctly. Choose a container that holds in your room and also leaves some space around the area so that you can maintain your hydroponics easily. Some large plants hang over the side of growing tanks, so you must consider that point before buying a hydroponic system.

When determining the size of the system, you need to consider accessibility too. There is no point in having a system that is so big you cannot get around it and access your plants and equipment.

If you are growing in an attic, then you need to consider the size of the entrance and whether the tank will fit. As roof height is a significant consideration in attic rooms, you may want to buy growing systems low to the ground. There is plenty of room for the plants to grow upwards.

How noisy is the System?

You may initially think this is a minor consideration. Still, when you have to live with the system continually making noise all day long, you may suddenly give this point more thought.

For larger systems, you will need a larger pump, which means more noise unless you are making your system up from multiple smaller units.

One thing to consider is when the pump will be running during the day. If it is loud, then you are not going to mind the noise during the day when you are at work, but running it at night is going to disturb you and your family. An NFT system needs the pump virtually 24 hours a day, whereas a flood and drain system is okay if the pump if on for a few minutes every two or three hours.

This is a stern judgment to make. It is worth visiting a store and looking at the different pumps to hear how noisy they are for yourself before making your decision.

Cost

Your budget is another primary consideration for you while choosing a hydroponic system. Many hydroponic systems like aeroponics come in ready-made kits. Still, they are usually expensive to buy and maintain as well. So, if you need a hydroponic system that will suit your budget, then you can buy some parts and assemble them on your own. Water culture hydroponics is a better option for you if you need an affordable hydroponics system that you can easily build on your own. All you need is to buy some everyday items like a water tank, air stone, bubble maker, a few cups to plant the system, gravel-like stone or sand, etc. Some of these items are readily available around your house, and you can use them in a hydroponics system.

Make a list of what you need for a hydroponics system and check whether any items are already available at your home. Do some research on the price of these items online and offline and choose the things that suit your budget.

This is a significant part of the decision-making process for many people. There are pre-made systems for pretty much any budget. Still, for someone who really wants to do hydroponics on a budget, then you are looking at making your own system from components or spare parts.

Most people will start with a smaller system, and then when they get hooked on this hobby, either increase the number of systems they run or buy a bigger system!

Shopping around and looking online will help you to save some money as you will often find better discounts from online retailers.

Electricity and Other Running Costs

Most hydroponics systems need electricity to run the air bubbler. You should also need a heater to control the temperature of your hydroponic if you are living in cold weather areas. You will also need a lighting system that requires electricity. Other considerations like maintaining the nutrients in your solution, replacing the solution, replacing growing mediums, etc. that you should bother about. If you think that your hydroponic is not cost-effective, you can switch to a different hydroponic system. However, this should not be your concern if you are building hydroponics as a hobby.

The majority of hydroponic systems will use electricity to power the pump and sometimes a nutrient heater in the colder months to keep the nutrient solution at the right temperature. For year-round production, you will need lights, which will use more electricity.

On top of that, you have to consider the other running costs like water, replacing the growing medium, nutrients, etc.

Can you Leave Your Hydroponic System?

Most hydroponic systems can be left unattended for a few days, depending on how big your nutrient reservoir is compared to the water needs of your plants. If you want to go to your plants for any length of time, you will need a good-sized nutrient container.

In most cases, you will change your nutrient solution around every two weeks and top it up every four or five days. The pH of it will need adjusting, and this can be done when topping it up.

Time and Manpower Needs

Different systems need different levels of attention from you. Some of the most expensive operations are mostly automated, meaning you don't need to do as much. In contrast, other systems require more frequent manual intervention. Will you be using pots or not?

Some of the growing systems allow you to grow in pots, which is excellent. You can use different growing mediums and adjust 'soil' conditions for individual plant requirements. This is helpful when you get started as you can grow a variety of other plants rather than only one type.

5.2 Summary - Before You Decide on a System

Before you start buying pre-made hydroponic systems or start setting up a DIY one, consider the type of plants that you will be growing. You will need to take the following into consideration:

1.   The size of the plant
2.   The size of the roots
3.   How the oxygen will reach the roots
•   How much water will the plants consume

5.   The maximum amount of space you have for a hydroponic system

6.   The nutrients that your plants will need to grow

7.   How your plants will get light

No matter which type of plants you are planning to grow, you will definitely want to

Build and design a hydroponic system that you will use more than once. With this in mind, you should first think about how you will harvest the crops in the future and then clean the system for the next batch of products that you are going to place in there. At the same time, you will also need to create a plan that will give you the allowances you require while your plants are still growing. That means that it should give you the space that you need when it comes to fixing problems that might arise without damaging the plants that are already in them.

Take note that any type of hydroponic system can be used for growing most types of plants if you design it in such a way that it will accommodate all needs that you can think of, even when the crops reach their full size. However, you may find that some crops may require less maintenance and funds if you grow them in another type of system instead, rather than trying to grow all of the crops that you have in mind in one large system.

Chapter 6: Types of Hydroponic Systems

One of the primary advantages of hydroponic farming is its versatility meaning that there is a large number of systems from which a farmer can choose from. The decision of which hydroponic system to choose is based on your needs, the plants you wish to grow, your budget, and the space you have set aside for the project.

6.1 Aeroponics

The aeroponics hydroponics system is the most high-tech of the possible setups, but this is not to mean that they are complicated: once you understand how the system works, the rest is easy. In this method, the plants' roots hang loose in the air and are occasionally sprayed with the nutrient concentrate. There are two ways to do it: using a pond flogger and using a spray nozzle to pour onto the roots. If you opt for a pond flogger, ensure that the flogger has been coated using Teflon because the coating makes it easier to maintain.

Some farmers time the misting cycles, just like the ebb and flow hydroponics system. The aeroponics cycle is much shorter because the misting's are only minutes apart. If you have an excellent sprayer, however, it is possible to mist the roots continuously so that an even more considerable amount of oxygen is available to the roots.

The use of the aeroponics systems has shown that plants grow even quicker using this method than the simpler systems like the deep-water culture. However, this is yet to be verified across the spectrum. In case you want to try this method out for yourself, ensure that you purchase finer sprayer nozzles than the typical ones, to help you atomize the solution.

The Advantages of Aeroponics

• exposing the roots increases their access to oxygen, which is unlike other methods that submerge the plants' root systems in the nutrient solution

• this method saves on nutrients, water, and the growing medium

• it is cost-effective and efficient, especially when you finish carrying out the initial setup

Disadvantages of Aeroponics

• at the very slightest interruption, suppose the high-pressure nozzles failed. The roots can dry out, and the effect can be even more severe than what would happen if you had the N.F.T. system setup.

• The timers and the pump need regular inspection, which causes the system to be quite demanding in maintenance.

• The aeroponics system is not as easy or cheap to set up as other methods are.

What You Would Need to Start an Aeroponics System as A DIY

• A solution reservoir

• PH kit

• Mist nozzles, sprinklers, or sprayers

• a fitted lid to keep the moisture in a submersible pump that has tubing whose ends have mist sprayers.

• a timer that will activate the sprayers at regular intervals

• A nutrient kit

6.2 Nutrient Film Technique (N.F.T.)

In these systems, the farmer grows his or her crops in tubes called gullies. Alternatively, the farmer can also use grow tanks to increase the speed at which the roots are growing. The gully, or the growing tray, must be placed above the reservoir at an angle. Ideally, a channel is created at the center of the grow tray so that it can be used to drain the solution with more efficiency.

The nutrient solution is pumped into the growing channels, and it runs along the bottom of the channel. However, when the solution gets to the end of the channel, it falls back into the main reservoir. The pump sends the solution back again to the beginning of the system. This movement creates a recirculating system, like the one used in deep water culture.

This system does not need a timer because the pump virtually ensures a constant supply of nutrients to the plant roots. The plants only need to be situated in their net pots. They do not require a growing medium; they are suspended in the air, just as in the aeroponics setup. However, in the N.F.T system, the plants can only be harvested or replaced one after the other.

The nutrient solution must be kept aerated by the use of an air pump and an air stone. The constant bubbling also helps to prevent the solution from settling while providing the roots with the oxygen they need to aid in the process of nutrient absorption, so that the plant will use less energy in sourcing for the nutrients it needs and more energy in growing and producing fruit.

Having a submersible pump at the reservoir ensures that the nutrient solution is continuously supplied to the grow tray.

Having a gap between the water and the plants also guarantees aeration before the water drains off into the reservoir. The NFT is undoubtedly an improvement of the drip system, as you shall see next.

The benefit of the N.F.T

● this technique is cost-effective because it does not require a growing medium. The nutrient solution that is used is often recycled and recovered back to the reservoir.

Disadvantages of the N.F.T

● the cost of maintenance, in this case, is higher because the pumps need regular supervision to ensure that they are working well as it should be.

● If there is an interruption of the power supply, the roots will dry out very quickly, mainly because it does not use any growing medium.

● Some roots tend to overgrow, and they clog the channels.

What You Would Need to Set Up an N.F.T System

● A nutrient kit

● a reservoir

● A pH kit

● Gullies or grow tanks, from which you grow the plants

● Tubes to direct the nutrient solution from the channel and into the reservoir tank

● Tubing and pump to direct the nutrient solution from the reservoir to the plants

● A spreader mat (this one is optional), to boost nutrient absorption

● a platform or a table to hold the gullies, together with a channel that can direct the nutrients back into the reservoir.

6.3 The Ebb and Flow Hydroponics System

The Ebb and Flow system, sometimes called the Flood, and Drain system is more advanced and more complicated than any other. The plants are placed in a grow tray in the growing medium and then placed at the top of the reservoir. There is also a scheduled timer, which causes the pump to switch on and flood the grow tray with the nutrient solution drawn from the pool at regular intervals. Once the grow tray floods, the timer switches off, and the nutrient solution drains off.

The Ebb and Flow hydroponics system are either set as a recovery or as a non-recovery system to mean that the solution could be used only once and discarded, or that it could be collected and reused.

The frequency of flooding for this method depends on factors like the amount of water that the plants need, the size of the plants, where your plants stand in the growth cycle, and the temperature in the air.

The flooding cycle is easy. It starts with having a water pump, the reservoir placed underneath the grow tray, and a timer to determine the frequency of flooding. Once you flood the tray, the law of gravity will order the excess solution back to the reservoir below, where it will be oxygenated by both the air stone and the air pump. The answer then sits in the pool, in readiness for the next flooding cycle.

Hydroponic farmers who choose the ebb and flow system do so for the flexibility of the system.

The system allows the tray to fill with the growing medium of choice, and for the farmers to organize their plants in net pots. They also get better control of the plants' roots.

Advantages of the Ebb and Flow Hydroponics System

- the system allows the efficient use of energy and water

- it can be customized to match your needs

- it is easy to control the temperature of the project because it is set up indoors and because the reservoir is differently placed from the growing trays.

- The plants enjoy good aeration because they are not fully submerged in the nutrient solution. At the same time, they get to enjoy the absorption of nutrients at regular times.

- Since the plants do not directly connect to the reservoir, it is possible to grow a larger proportion of crops than the pool can hold.

Disadvantages of the Ebb and Flow Hydroponics System

- The system uses a great deal of the growing media

- In case of a power supply disruption, the pumps and the timers will be affected, causing the roots to dry up. However, this problem can be resolved by merely choosing mediums that ideally take in and efficiently retain moisture.

- A farmer needs to have some level of experience maintaining the pH and nutrient levels and to ensure that the system, including the medium, does not clog with the salts contained in the nutrient solution.

6.4 Drip Irrigation System

The drip irrigation system is one of the more popular hydroponic systems. The system is set up to enable the transportation of nutrients from the reservoir using a tube down to an irrigation pipe that waters the plant's base.

Drip irrigation may recover the nutrient solution, or not. Home growers tend to lean towards recovery while commercial growers lean towards non-recovery.

Advantages of the Drip System

- A relatively cheap method

- the farmer has greater control of the watering and feeding schedule

- less likely to break down

- it is possible to set the timers so precisely that the plants will be let until when more of the solution is needed

Disadvantages of the Drip System

- for a small garden, a drip system is slightly overkill

- The nutrients and pH levels tend to fluctuate, especially when using a recirculating system

- there is a high level of waste, especially if using a non-recovery method

- If the farmer takes the non-recovery option, the cost of purchasing nutrients may get so high

What You Need to Set Up the Drip Irrigation System

- a timer

- PH kit

- growing medium

- Containers or growing trays for the plants

- Reservoir container to house the nutrient solution

- The air pump that contains air stones and tubing

- Drip lines and irrigation pipes with sets of joiners and adapters

- Nutrient kit

- Submersible pump and tubing to deliver the nutrients

6.5 The Wick System

The wick system is naturally passive. There are no moving parts that require automation, and hence no electricity is needed to run activities and functions. This makes the wick system a perfect selection for just getting their feet wet and those working with a tight budget.

The wick system is the simplest of them all. It works by causing the plant to receive nutrients using a wick attached to the reservoir on one end, and the plant on the other end. When the end in the pool soaks up, it transports the nutrient solution through the fiber of the wick, on to the plant.

One trick for succeeding in using a wick system is to use a growing media that can transport nutrients and water well. Some of the excellent options you may choose from include perlite, coconut coir, and vermiculite.

Advantages of the Wick System

- Easy to set up

- An excellent pick for beginners and children

- Affordable

- Once you have set it up correctly, this is a genuinely hands-off method

- the wick system is especially suited for small plants, those with lesser nutritional needs

Disadvantages of the Wick System

- is not suited to larger plants that have higher nutrient requirements because they may need much more moisture and nutrient than the wick can deliver

- The wick system does not make the process of controlling the humidity of the growing room easy

- the system may cause uneven absorption of nutrients, and with time, there could be a buildup of nutrients in the growing medium

- if the wick is improperly placed, it could mean death for your crops

What You Would Need to Set Up a Wick System

- A nutrient kit

- A bucket, reservoir, or just a tub with a lid

- some growing medium

- Basket or container

- a wick could be a rope or any other absorbent material

6.6 The Deep-Water Culture System

The deep-water culture system is the simplest of them all. It is a system in which many plants are placed on a tray, ideally made of polystyrene, which then floats at the top of the nutrient solution that has been held in a solution reservoir. In this setup, the plant's roots will be completely submerged in the water.

Instead of the polystyrene sheet, the plants can also be placed in net pots, and the pots can be fitted into a lid that will fit the circumference of the reservoir, tank, or tub in use.

An air stone connected to an air pump is used to keep the nutrient solution below oxygenated, which ensures that the plants' roots do not become waterlogged to the point that they would rot and be incapable of absorbing the nutrients below.

Plants best suited for this setup include Asian greens, lettuce, endives, and rocket, among others.

Advantages of the Deep-Water Culture System

- Affordable

- Easy to build
- Management is easy
- Requires only a small space
- Suited for beginners
- Suitable for commercial hydroponics farming
- Ideal for plants with short growing periods
- Less wastage because the system reuses the same nutrient solution

Disadvantages of Deep-Water Culture System

- not suited for large plants
- Not suited to plants that have long growing periods

What You Need to Set Up the Deep-Water Culture System

- Air pump
- System-specific reservoirs
- PH kit
- Nutrient kit
- Airstone
- Air pump
- growing medium

The above systems are the six major hydroponics systems types. You can clearly read how each works and the advantages and disadvantages of each system.

Do not be anxious about which method you choose, though, because no matter the method you choose, provided you provide proper care.

Your plants will grow very big and very fast. With any of these systems, you will assuredly experience the ups that hydroponics offer, particularly the flexibility, so that whenever you are having trouble, you will have no reservations about correcting them and getting your farm back on the right track.

6.7 Advanced Hydroponic Systems

The above six hydroponics systems are best suited for beginners. For your knowledge, we will discuss three more hydroponic systems in brief, so that you do not confuse between the beginners' and advanced kind.

The systems include:

6.8 The Kratky Method

The Kratky method is one that combines the deep-water culture system and the wick system. It brings in the constant adequate supply advantage of the deep-water culture system added to the passivity and low maintenance of the wick system.

In the Kratky method, the plants are held in a net pot, on top of an anon-circulating solution reservoir with a tight-fitting lid. The net pot is fitted into a hole that has been cut out of the cover. At first, the roots are submerged beneath the solution, and only a small air gap is left between the nutrient solution and the inside of the lid.

Once this is done, the farmer then leaves the system alone. As the plant and the growing medium absorb the right nutrients, the roots of the plant grow, the water level falls, and the space between the solution and the inside of the lid gets bigger.

This space ensures that the plant receives the nutrition it needs from the solution while getting enough oxygen supply.

Advantages

- this method can be the right way for beginners to get into hydroponics farming

- it almost requires zero maintenance

- the method is affordable

Disadvantages

- only suited for small foliage crops

- Not ideal for large scale farming

6.9 Fogponics

Fogponics is a tremendous improvement of aeroponics, evidenced by the improved farming results. Fogponics has improved farming rapidly.

It works this way: rather than creating a mist at specified intervals, the farmer installs a fogger in the reservoir to create a humidified environment. The fogger, or the mist maker, as you can tell, changes the size of water droplets to the point that they become a mist or fog, which is then directed to the plants' root system.

The new gravity-defying nutrient solution droplets offer the plant a full nutrient coverage to the point that it stimulates the development of new root hairs as an adaptation to increase the surface area of the root system, for greater absorption of the nutrients.

Advantages of the Fogponics System

- Reduces the water and nutrients usage by more than 40 percent

- Economical

- Easy to set up

- The nutrient solution does not reduce in concentration because the recirculation is not used up.

Disadvantages of Fogponics

- The cost of the initial setup is relatively high

- The mist is very light, yet it must be contained

- In case there is a power outage, the havoc wreaked to the crops can be ridiculously big

- The setup requires regular cleaning of the equipment, and this increases the cost of maintenance

Chapter 7: Layout Of Hydroponic Structure

7.1 Step By Step Instructions To Assemble A Homemade Hydroponic System

Decide the Location

Find the hydroponic system in an encased structure, such as a nursery or the storm cellar of your home, or on an open-air porch or deck. The floor ought to be level to guarantee even the inclusion of water and nutrients to the plants in the system. On the off chance that setting the system outside, shield the system from the components, for example, giving a breeze obstruction, and check the water levels all the more regularly because of water misfortune from vanishing. During cold temperatures, bring the hydroponic system inside. If it is putting the system in an inside room of your home, add the develop lights to give supplemental lighting to the plants.

Stage 1: Assemble the Hydroponic System

The system comprises six growing cylinders made of 6" PVC pipe, a stand and trellis made of PVC, a 50-gallon supplement tank, a siphon, and a complex. The tank sits under the table of 6" PVC growing cylinders. The siphon sits inside the tank to drive nutrients up to the plants using a complex of littler PVC channels and plastic cylinders. Each growing cylinder has a drainpipe that leads back to the tank. The complex sits over the channels and sends pressurized water to the cylinders.

Water is pushed through a square of PVC to get the nutrients to the plants in this system, the complex, and afterward gets shot out to little plastic cylinders that run inside every one of the bigger growing cylinders.

The supplement tubes have tiny openings in them, one gap between each plant site. The nutrients shoot out the gap and shower the plant roots. Simultaneously, the stream of water makes air bubbles, so the plants get enough oxygen.

Stage 2: Mix the Nutrients and Water in the Tank

Fill the 50-gallon tank with water. At that point, add two cups of nutrients to the tank (or as prescribed by the manure mark), turn on the siphon, and let the system run for around 30 minutes to get the entirety of the nutrients altogether blended.

Stage 3: Add Plants to the Growing Tubes

Probably the most effortless approach to plant a hydroponic nursery is to utilize acquired seedlings, particularly on the off chance that you don't have the opportunity to develop the seeds yourself. The key is to pick the most beneficial plants you can discover and afterward evacuate the entirety of the soil off their underlying foundations. To wash the soil off the roots, submerge the root ball in a pail of lukewarm to cold water. Water that is excessively warm or too cold can send the plant into stun — tenderly isolated the roots to get the soil out. Any soil left on the roots could obstruct the small shower openings in the supplement tubes.

After the roots are spotless, pull the same number of roots as you can through the base of the planting cup and afterward add extended mudrocks to hold the plant set up and upstanding. The extended soil rocks are hard, but on the other hand, they're exceptionally light with the goal that they don't harm the plant roots.

Stage 4: Tie the Plants to the Trellis

Utilize the plant clasps and string to attach the plants to the trellis. The string will give them backing to climb straight up, amplifying the space in this kept region.

Bind the string freely to the highest point of the trellis, append the clasps and string to each plant (Image 2) and delicately wind the tips of the plants around the string.

Stage 5: Turn on the Pump and Monitor the System Daily

Check the water levels every day; in specific locales, it might be essential to check it two times per day, contingent upon water misfortune because of over the top warmth and vanishing. Check the pH and supplement levels at regular intervals. Since the siphon runs full time, you needn't bother with a clock, yet ensure the tank doesn't dry out, or the siphon will catch fire.

Stage 6: Monitor Plant Growth

Half a month in the wake of planting, the plants will cover the trellis since they'll have all the water and nutrients they have to develop rapidly. It's imperative to watch out for plant development and tie or clasp the plant stalks like clockwork.

Stage 7: Inspect for Pests and Diseases

Search for indications of pests and diseases, for example, the nearness of creepy-crawly pests, bit leaves, and foliar diseases. One diseased plant can quickly contaminate the various ones since they are so near one another. Evacuate any debilitated plants right away. Since plants developed hydroponically don't need to spend their vitality attempting to discover nourishment, they can invest more energy growing. This encourages them to be more advantageous and more grounded because they can utilize a portion of that vitality to ward off diseases. Since the leaves of the plants never get wet except if it downpours, they're substantially less liable to get leaf growth, buildup, and shape.

Although hydroponic plants are great at warding off diseases, regardless, they need to battle pests.

Irrespective of whether it's hydroponic, creepy crawlies and caterpillars can all things considered to discover a route into the nursery. Take out and discard any bugs you see.

7.2 Picking The Best Hydroponics Equipment

If you are keen on hydroponic gardening, you should utilize the best hardware to get an opportunity for accomplishment. Contingent upon your degree of experience, accessible spending plan, and gardening needs, you can pick one of the numerous kinds of hydroponic systems accessible. Nonetheless, as you will see, a portion of the fundamental bits of hardware used to fabricate various systems are comparative.

Picking the best of fundamental hydroponics gear, as controlled by your particular gardening prerequisites, will help make crafted by exceeding expectations at hydroponics a lot simpler. Here's a breakdown of the most significant hydroponics gear utilized in many systems, joined by some helpful hints on the most proficient method to pick the best of each.

The Reservoir

The repository utilized in hydroponic systems holds the water that has the nutrients to be provided to your plants. As the essential segment of any hydroponic system, the supply holds the water expected to keep your plants flooded with dampness and minerals.

Contingent upon your financial limit, just as the size of your activity, the store can be anything from a costly business variation or a central basin.

To anticipate the vanishing of the water held in that, which would influence the supplement balance, make sure to pick a repository that accompanies a cover.

Besides, the best store ought not to be metallic as it might prompt the presentation of destructive minerals into the supplement arrangement, or the event of concoction responses that may wind up harming your plants.

Water Pump

To supply your plants with the water and minerals they have to endure, and you have to get your hands on a dependable water siphon. The two fundamental sorts of water siphons are submersible and non-submersible. The previous is introduced in the supplement arrangement while the last should be introduced outside the arrangement. Water siphons are additionally arranged by their yield in Gallons Per Minute (GPM) or Gallons Per Hour (GPH). On the off chance that you have a little setup, at that point, a siphon that conveys around 30 to 40 GPH will have the option to supply your plants with the water they need, and won't cost a lot.

Make sure likewise to consider the rate at which water channels from the develop media while picking a water siphon that meets the ideal degree of yield.

Clock

In most hydroponic systems, aside from the most major ones, a clock must help with the guideline of various essential capacities. For example, a watch can be utilized to manage watering, ventilation, and lighting cycles. While picking the best clock for your system, you will have two principle decisions, less difficult and increasingly reasonable simple units or costlier, further developed advanced units. The last is best for those hoping to make a system for growing sensitive plants that require the most extreme exactness during the execution of every activity.

Lighting

To upgrade the development of your plants, you have to have the privilege to develop lights. It is essential to specify now that even though glaring lights can be utilized to enhance normal light, they can't, all alone, give the range of light required by plants. Metal Halide and High-Pressure Sodium Lights were created to radiate a variety of light that impersonates the nature of light exuding from the sun. Metal Halide lights are the nearest you can get to daylight. They produce increasingly a greater extent of blue light that is incredible for supporting vegetative development.

High weight sodium lights then again produce light that spreads a greater amount of the red-orange range. They last more, consume more splendid, and expend a lower measure of vitality than their metal halide partners, even though they produce a smaller range of light. For the best outcomes, it is prescribed that you consolidate the utilization of the two sorts of lights to give light that is as close as conceivable to the full range of daylight. Besides, you can utilize light reflectors and movers to cover a more extensive space with fewer lights.

Development Media

The soil has no spot in hydroponics; idle, non-natural materials are utilized in its place. The development of media is utilized to help the plant as it develops. The medium picked ought to notwithstanding tying down the plants, encourage appropriate seepage and air circulation of the roots. Polyurethane froth, perlite, bark, rock, vermiculite, and coconut fiber are a portion of your primary alternatives here. The correct development medium ought to be sufficiently thick to stay the plant yet less that it impedes the flow of air and the supplement arrangement.

The particles of the medium ought to have the option to hold dampness and nutrients sufficiently long to permit the roots to retain the important degree of nutrients in the middle of flooding. At long last, it ought to be sterile to avoid the engendering of diseases, pests, and parasites.

pH Test Kit

You have to keep up the pH equalization of the supplement answers to get any opportunity of growing a solid hydroponic nursery. Although a few plants might have the option to develop soundly at a lower or higher pH level, it is prescribed that you keep it at somewhere in the range of 6 and 6.5. This implies you need to obtain a pH test unit. Of all the hydroponic hardware examined over, these units are the most reasonable, yet also among the most significant. Growing a hydroponic nursery includes less work than growing a nursery in the soil. Be that as it may, to succeed, you have to have the best hydroponics hardware from the beginning, paying little heed to whether you decide to go with an instant pack or are anticipating assembling your special system a tiny bit at a time.

7.3 Building a Homemade Hydroponics System

Utilizing hydroponics systems will enable your plants to develop about half quicker than they would in standard soil. Hydroponics likewise yields better gathers since nutrients are conveyed straightforwardly to the plants. Utilizing hydroponics is an ideal coach to cultivate for city inhabitants like us without any stresses over soil and space - only the plants! In building your very own hydroponics system at home, you will require these essential materials. You will need a supply, pots - made of nets or work, a growing medium, supplement arrangement, air stones, carriers or tubing, and a pneumatic machine. You additionally need some Styrofoam, a sharp blade or box shaper, and a measuring tape.

The first activity is to pick a decent repository. You can utilize a pail, fish tank, a receptacle, or any holder as long as it fits all your prospected number of pots for your plants. You will likewise need to paint the container dark; this is fundamental just if your store is straightforward. In such a case that light is permitted in it, this advances green growth and different risky that is awful for your plants.

Next, draw a straight line down the side of the storage tank to fill in as check-in observing water or supplement arrangement level. At that point, measure your tank utilizing the measuring tape, get the measurements, and start to cut the Styrofoam into pieces that are one-fourth of an inch littler than the size of the supply and fit it inside. This will be your floater and ought to be over the supplement arrangement and acclimate to water level changes.

Presently, cut gaps where you can put your pots. Spot them equitably over the Styrofoam, ensuring sufficient space for each to get enough daylight. Make another gap on any end for the air to go through uninhibitedly. Get your pneumatic machine and associate the free finish of the tubing to the air stone. Set your system up by filling the store with the supplement arrangement. Run the tubing through the end gap of the Styrofoam and spot it in the store. Presently, fill the pots with the growing medium and plant the seeds in. Put them on the floater. Turn on the siphon and voila! You are done.

In reality, you can buy hydroponics or develop units at shops on the web and approach you. Most units have everything! They incorporate gardening supplies and essential materials like seeds, nutrients, growing medium, and different enhancements. Some may include channels, siphons, growing plates, stores, and other segments depending truly on what specific hydroponics system you decide to introduce.

Chapter 8: Planting in Containers

8.1 How To Grow Carrots In Containers

Have you been attempting to develop perfect straight carrots that are not stubby or forked? For a long time, my endeavors to grow carrots have been loaded with disappointment. Where I live, the dirt is of mud, despite working it to an excellent consistency; regardless, it causes me issues. As of late, I've perused some interesting articles on the best way to develop whole carrots unfailingly, and here I will impart what I've learned.

As I got some free 'Early Nantes 2' seed from a cultivating magazine, this is the thing that I will depend on to bring me achievement this year.

Carrots do best in red, sandy, and well-depleting soil. So, to re-make this, I will develop my carrots in containers to recreate their perfect conditions. The bottles need a depth of 30 cm to enable the carrots to become long and a width of 20 cm to give a decent spread.

Combine one-third of old preparing fertilizer with one-third of good quality fresh preparing manure and 33% of vermiculite.

As carrot seeds are little, it is anything but challenging to plant too much. Blend the seed with sand before sowing, and afterward, dissipate over the outside of the manure in your container. Press down lightly and give a light watering.

Carrots take around 15 - 20 days to sprout at a temperature of 10 degrees Celsius or more. Along these lines, to give carrots a head start, you have to develop them in a greenhouse. If you don't have a greenhouse, you can generally grow them in the shed or on a kitchen windowsill where they will get a lot of light. When the days are hotter, the pots can be taken outside to stand

When the seedlings are about 25mm tall, begin the dispensing procedure. As they are very fragile at this stage, utilize a couple of tweezers or a little pair of sharp scissors. Cut the stems of the carrot seedlings just underneath the surface. You need to leave plants appropriated at 5cm interims. Keep in mind to keep the fertilizer watered to keep the carrots from drying out as your carrots become ever more prominent. If you need to maintain a strategic distance from green tops, strain some manure over the highest point of them.

Developing Carrots in a Container

Carrots are one vegetable I am always conscious about whether to grow or not. They can be tricky and are inclined to carrot fly. However, once you have tasted the fantastic flavor you get from homegrown carrots, that is ordinarily enough to influence my decision to grow my own. Carrots are regularly sown into the ground and require a light, very much depleted the soil, so utilizing containers to develop them is a perfect option.

Another valid justification for developing carrots in a container is that, when grown in the ground, carrots can be effectively contorted by stones or large bunches of soil going about as impediments. They are additionally inclined to assault via carrot fly, yet if you utilize an expansive container or spot around two feet off the ground, it will help discourage them as carrot fly typically flies down and out.

Picking a container

Pick a container that isn't too shallow to allow the carrots to put down great roots. Its size will rely upon what number of carrots you need to collect; however, for a decent yield, you will require a genuinely expansive pot or even a few. The material is likewise, imperative. Also, though earthenware looks pleasant, it warms up rapidly and, in this way, loses a great deal of dampness, and you will end up losing water all the more frequently. As I would see it, a decent measured plastic pot carries out the responsibility pleasantly.

Sowing the carrots

Fill your picked container with multi-use manure and water well. Throw around half of a bundle of carrot seed into a little bowl of either sand or vermiculite.

Blending the seed along these lines will assist you with an even circulation as carrot seed is small and straightforward to sow too much.

When you have sprinkled your seed over the manure, spread the top with a thin layer of fertilizer. Regardless of whether you are cautious while sowing carrot seed, you will find that, once the seed rises, you should disperse the seedlings. Keep your carrots watered, and in half a month, you ought to have the capacity to begin reaping scrumptious baby carrots.

Carrot assortments

There are many assortments of carrot. If you are puzzled by the decision, I will choose Marion or Resistively. Marion is appropriate for lasting throughout the year, and the roots are exceptionally delicate. Resistively is a primary yield carrot with decent protection from carrot fly, as its name recommends. All can be designed expertly in a patio nursery grower.

8.2 How To Grow Lettuce In Containers

If you need to grow your very own vegetables but don't have much space for it, selecting plants that can be grown in containers can be your most reliable option. In this case, learning how to grow lettuce is one of the most straightforward approaches.

Besides this, lettuce has an exceptional nutritional value, making it a standout amongst the most widely recognized vegetables grown by natural home growers. It is rich in nutrients A, K, and C, just as cancer prevention agents and beta carotene. Also, if you're attached to salad, there's no better and fresher approach to set up your mixture than to utilize the produce from your very own little greenhouse.

Growing lettuce may not be quite a bit of trouble, but instead, there are several things you have to remember to guarantee that you'll grow excellent lettuce. A portion of these things are:

Readiness of Containers

First things first, you have to discover ideal containers you can use for your little greenery enclosure. You can utilize window boxes, planters, planters, or even the holder used in many grocery stores to display lettuce or different natural products or vegetables. When you locate a suitable compartment, you have to make a few cuts on its base to allow for water flow when watering the plants.

The following stage would include setting up the soil you're going to place inside the containers. The best soil type, for this reason, would be humus soil. You could also include a fair bit of perlite and vermiculite. Both will help in the best possible ingestion of air and water along these lines, assisting in the ideal growth of your plants.

Planting the Seeds

When the containers are prepared, you can begin sowing the lettuce seed. Make sure to utilize high seeds from trusted brands. The seeds must be planted with a profundity of 1/4 of an inch. After sowing, splash with water gently.

The seeds will grow for around 1 or 2 weeks. After watching growth, you can disperse the lettuce, allowing additional room for the lusher ones. You have the alternative of transplanting the seedlings you have removed from the containers.

Care and Maintenance

With appropriate consideration, you can hope to collect fresh lettuce from your little greenery enclosure at any time of the year. Merely guarantee that the elements required by the plants are met. For example, lettuce must be watered regularly. However, it must be so that it will just keep up the sogginess of the soil.

Also, lettuce would expect an introduction to light. It might require 10-12 hours of light submission. Notwithstanding, while presenting it to sunlight, you need to remember that lettuce grows best in more relaxed situations. This is the reason you also need to make sure the temperature doesn't get excessively high.

Additionally, placing manure rich in nitrogen, potassium, and phosphorus will help in delivering top-notch lettuce.

8.3 How To Grow Basil In Containers

Basil is a useful ingredient in many Italian recipes, such as salads, sandwiches, and dishes. Along these lines, it makes sense that figuring out how to grow basil is a sure-fire approach to guarantee you generally have a new supply to use in your cooking.

For whatever length of time, you have great light and the correct temperature, growing basil is exceptionally simple. You can grow basil effectively from seeds or buy an "herb pack" with all you need. In any case, a bundled unit isn't necessary; all you need are basil seeds and some fertile soil.

Basil needs to grow in soil that is legitimately depleted, so you should make sure to get a holder that has excellent waste. Search for planters or pots with significant gaps, or you can put a few stones, rock, and shakes at the base to contain the water.

Remember that basil won't endure ice if you are planting it outside. The seeds are little, yet most will grow, and the seedlings can be dispersed later if necessary, so don't be hesitant to plant a few in one pot. If you are utilizing a holder, sprinkle the seeds gently with soil and water with a splash bottle.

If you are figuring out how to grow basil, remember that the plants will require six to eight hours of sun every day. Inside, the plant should be put in a radiant window, and outside you have to ensure the plant has sun for most of the day, yet that it is out of the breeze.

Basil plants should be watered a few times each week. They should additionally be prepared every month. Attempt to keep the water at the base of the plant, so it enables growths to set in.

As blooms show up on your basil plant, expel them by squeezing them off. In that manner, the plant utilizes its vitality to deliver delicious leaves rather than blossoms, giving you the most delightful item.

The benefit of figuring out how to grow basil is that you will most likely always have the fresh herb for use whenever you wish. You can grow it through the year by planting it in compartments inside your home. It's a smart thought to have a few plants close by at one time. Collect the leaves at the highest point of the plant at whatever point you wish to utilize them, and your plants ought to be profitable for a long time.

The most effective method to Grow Basil

Today there are splashes, scented candles, modules, and even plates that guarantee to refresh your air by putting an assortment of smells into your home.

In any case, when you realize how to grow basil, you can have enough variety of aroma to bundle your very own blend! The most usually grown basil is the yearly, Osmium basilica that conveys a minty scent that smells like sweet basil. Notwithstanding having a superb fragrance, fresh basil is a fundamental fixing in soups, stews, pesto sauce, and pretty much any tomato dish.

Realizing how to grow basil is an absolute necessity for each herb plant specialist. You can grow herbs both inside and outside.

Basil comes in more than 160 assortments that, notwithstanding the sweet basil scent, offer different fragrances like those of lemon, licorice, and cinnamon and foliage hues that go from emerald green to imperial purple. Figure out how to grow basil, and you give a treat to your eyes and a fragrant treat for your nose.

By and large, when figuring out how to grow basil, you'll need to begin your plants from seeds. Until basil stems are almost adult, they are very delicate and effectively broken and wounded, so transplanting youthful basil cultivars can be a pointless activity. Fortunately, basil is one of the varieties that can be seeded into your greenhouse. If you reseed your basil plot at regular intervals, you'll have fresh basil throughout the entire summer.

Basil is a low-upkeep plant. Even though it inclines toward the full sun, it will grow in partial shade. When seedlings are set up, basil is additionally dry season tolerant. It will give you a better flavor if you don't treat it! One tip you should think about how to grow basil and safeguard its full character for culinary use is to squeeze off bloom spikes as they form.

Some portion of the enjoyment of learning how to grow basil is the full range of approaches to save it after collection. You can gather your basil anytime by cutting off its leaves as you need them. They transform numerous ordinary dishes into indulgences when utilized new. Basil can likewise be dried by cutting a few stems and draping them in packs together.

Air-drying basil along these lines is an excellent method to add its smell to your kitchen! When your basil groups are dry, you can disintegrate the leaves and store them in glass bottles.

Basil can likewise be saved by solidifying. Stop small amounts of fresh basil in plastic packs or chop them and stop them in water in an ice-solid shape plate.

Basil is a simple growing herb brimming with conceivable outcomes for a home stylistic theme, scent, and culinary use. Also, it's appropriate for compartment growing for direct seeding into your greenery enclosure. Figuring out how to grow basil is a sweetly fulfilling piece of planting, regardless of what assortment you grow!

Chapter 9: Trouble Shooting Hydroponics System Problems

If you've quite recently set up or are presently running a hydroponics garden, you will, in the long run, have an issue and need to do some investigating hydroponics framework work. Generally, however, it's not as huge an issue as it would appear. In case you're utilizing a pre-made pack, however, it can appear to be troublesome since you didn't assemble it yourself, so you probably won't be as acquainted with the parts as you would somehow or another be.

That is as yet not a serious deal, however. All hydroponics systems work in a similar fundamental manner. Almost the entirety of their segments is the equivalent when you come it down. When you understand that reality and realize what those systems are and how they work, inconvenience shooting and fixing are certifiably not a genuine worry.

In light of the entirety of that, we should experience the fundamentals of a hydroponics framework and afterward take a gander at some normal issues and solutions for one that is breaking down.

Initial, a regular hydroponics garden will comprise of five fundamental parts: the plate (or "beds"), a flow framework for the nutrient solution, a grow light (or lights), and a suspension framework or mode for the plants' support. The fifth part is simply the plants, obviously.

Basic issues with hydroponic gardens as a rule rotate around the nutrient solution or the flow framework. So much of the time, inconvenience shooting hydroponics framework issues revolve around these two components.

Plants Sickly or Withering

On the off chance that your plants are getting debilitated, starting to shrivel, or aren't doing admirably something else, at that point, your concern is likely in one of two places: the nutrient solution and its dissemination or the light being given.

Clearly, if it's the last mentioned, you'll have to either build, lessening, or move the lighting. "Consumed" or "seared" plants mean the light is excessively close (it ought to be at any rate six to eight inches from the leaves, according to the light producer's suggestions).

Something else, your issues are in the nutrient solution. Ensure that it's flowing appropriately. See that it's going into the medium (or solution plate) and traveling through to the channel without impediment. Here and there, the media will "bunch" or have plant parts or different barricades upsetting the progression of nutrient solution. In case you're utilizing extended mud or coir, be sure it's not stopped up with extra roots from past plantings-a typical issue with these mediums.

The solution itself ought to be checked for pH level utilizing a testing scoop or short test strips. Now and again, particularly as the plants experience their quickest growth periods (shortly before development), they will emit more squanders than something else. This can mean the solution is over-immersed with blows, prompting higher acidity levels. This is cured with a straightforward weakening of water or substitution of the nutrient solution through and through (best).

Nutrient Solution Not Circulating

The response to this issue is likely the undeniable one: is the siphon working? Something else, the above checks for the clear stream will likely discover the problem.

Green growth or Parasite Infestation

This is additionally a typical issue, particularly for profound water cultures. Green growth frequently starts to grow on the sides of tanks or in the hoses interfacing the solution dissemination supply, siphon, and so on. The simple fix for most green growth issues is to limit its entrance to daylight. Tanks, plate, etc. should be dull (store-obtained units are frequently dark green or dark) to square daylight invasion. If they aren't, dark trash backs can be utilized to line the inside or out to hinder the light and carry out the responsibility.

Parasites are another issue that can happen when the sterility of the framework is undermined. Outdoor/nursery systems regularly have a problem with this. The typical parasite executioners for gardening will work, either substance or physical. A characteristic or organic strategies like diatomaceous earth or vinegar solution is most suggested, obviously.

General Maintenance to Prevent Problems

Numerous issues with hydroponic systems originate from more seasoned hardware coming up short and from inappropriate upkeep. Make sure to keep up your framework to shield this from occurring. It's not exceptionally troublesome, mainly if you make a propensity for it. The regularly ignored obligation is a thorough cleaning of the whole arrangement between crops.

When the beds are vacant, and the solution has been dumped, utilize a thorough cleaning strategy to flush out the cylinders, plate, medium, and so on. In all honesty, this flushing is like how you wipe out a trickle espresso creator. A 1:5 vinegar-water solution goes through a few times will carry out the responsibility. Simple!

More often than not, inconvenience shooting hydroponics framework issues is genuinely necessary since hydroponics isn't as perplexing as individuals who've never done it may think.

Chapter 10: Hydroponics Nutrient Guide

The requirements of a plant in any environment are the same – organic compost (C.O.N.H), micro, and macronutrients. Nevertheless, plants grown in hydroponic systems do not receive the necessary nutrients they need in similar ways.

For plants to survive and grow well, they need the following:

- Water
- Carbon Dioxide
- Lights
- Oxygen
- Nutrients

Plants receive carbon dioxide and oxygen from the environment for respiration. They get energy from lights, life, which is used in photosynthesis to make foods. Lights are supplied by either naturally from the sun or artificial lights from grow-bulbs. Water provides moisture to the plants.

Nutrients in the water are what you have absolute control over as a soilless grower to allow plants to get to their full potential growth. These are what I'm about discussing.

10.1 Macronutrients

What plants need in large amounts to thrive are Macronutrients.

Nitrogen

The primary food that plants need to grow is nitrogen, especially the vegetative growth stage. If there is no nitrogen, there will no leaves produced. Most importantly, it plays a crucial role in:

- Stem and leaf growth as well as its sizes and colors
- Amino acids, chlorophyll, protein synthesis, and co-enzymes.

Phosphorus (P)

Phosphorus is one of the elements of DNA, the genetic memory plants unit that plays an essential role in plant vigor and production of seed, and is also vital for photosynthesis. Plants need large amounts of Phosphorus at the early phase of sprouting, germinating, and flowering stage. Consequently, it's responsible for the formation of:

- Roots
- Flowering
- Seeds
- Fruits

Potassium (K)

This nutrient is useful in every phase of the plant's growth. It helps in synthesizing carbohydrates, starches, and sugar. Potassium also plays a vital role in the growth of flowers, roots, and stems. Plants that have enough Potassium will have useful insects and bacterial resistance.

Calcium (Ca)

Fast-growing vegetables and flowers require calcium almost as much as macronutrients. This is vital for the development and formation of the cell.

Magnesium (Mg)

Fast-growing plants also require large amounts of magnesium. And it is crucial to the production of chlorophyll. It helps in creating oxygen during photosynthesis, and this can be recognized in vigorous and healthy plants.

Sulfur

Sulfur is the component of twenty-one amino acids that form several hormones, protein, and vitamins, such as vitamin B.

10.2 Micro Nutrients

Smaller amounts of micronutrients are needed. However, they still play vital roles in the growth of plants.

Zinc

Zinc work with other components to form chlorophyll, which is vital for the growth of stem and good catalyst for most plant's enzymes.

Manganese

Manganese aids in the utilization of nitrogen alongside iron in chlorophyll production.

Iron

Iron is required for chlorophyll synthesis and also essential to the enzyme system.

Boron

Boron is combined with Calcium for cell membranes and chlorophyll formation.

These are not a complete list of micronutrients. But firstly pay attention to the macronutrients; once you do not give too much and deficient of these elements to the plants, you will be doing just fine.

Nonetheless, getting to understand all the needed nutrients for plant growth is not sufficient in reality. Some nutrients are only soluble at various levels of pH.

10.3 How does pH affect the Availability of Nutrients?

Different nutrients are available at a different level of Ph. Generally, macronutrients are soluble in the center of the lines. Meanwhile, micronutrients, which are trace elements, are available mostly in the middle level of pH, and some are at the lower left of the pH level.

You will notice that there is a sweet spot. That is a little left of the pH chart, namely from 5.5 to 6.5. So the usual rule of thumb for plants to absorb necessary nutrients is to keep your solution at this level.

10.4 How to Mix Nutrient Solutions

Any newbie to Hydroponics is advised to start with a recognized, already made nutrient-package for their own hydroponic gardening. If you want the nutrient step to be easy and also save time, it is ideal sticking with the available hydroponic nutrient products from your local garden center. When you have gathered some experiences, you can make your nutrient mix.

Generally, it is observed that the listed formula and ingredients of the solutions at the local stores are three numbers in percentage. And they are the three most vital nutrients that were mentioned above - Potassium (K), Phosphorus (P), and Nitrogen (N). For instance, they are available at the ratio 10-10-10; this implies that each nutrient contains 10% of the solution. The remaining seventy-percent are micro-nutrients, water, and other minerals that aid the nutritional process.

For sure, that ratio would be different, depending on varied factors:

- Types of plant

- Growth stage of plant

- Plants' you want to bring the most productions (root, fruit, or leaf)

- The period of the year, temperature, weather, and light intensity

Below are the recommended nutrient solutions for some types of plant:

Plant	N	P	K	Ca	Mg
Concentration in mg/ (ppm)					
Cucumber	200	4028014040			
Melon	200	4528511530			
Pepper	190	4528513040			
Roses	170	4528512040			
Strawberry	50	25	1506520		
Tomato	190	4031015045			

When you're to choose pre-made solutions for your system, remember to opt for the nutrient prepared specially for only hydroponics. Do not buy an all-purpose package that can be used in both hydroponics and soil gardening. The regular fertilizers used in traditional gardens don't have the necessary nutrients that hydroponics plants need.

Secondly, we recommend the use of two or three parts solution in the liquid. Typically it's easier to work with liquid solutions than that of powder type as it quickly absorbs in water and nearly all the liquid solution composts of pH buffers.

Also, it is ideal to purchase the three parts. Since it helps you later when you need to combine and blend different mixtures for the plant's growth and specific phase of development.

To save your time, here are easy steps to combine the 3 part solutions:

- Firstly, confirm the growth stages of your plants so as to mix the three parts with the right proportion. Check the instruction given by the producer of your nutrient products.

- Begin by adding clean water to the tank.

- Follow by adding the micronutrient to the water. It includes elements like boron calcium, manganese, iron, zinc, copper, and some nitrogen. Blend the solution.

- The growing part is the next. It composes of magnesium, nitrate nitrogen, potassium, phosphate, and ammoniacal nitrogen. And then stir thoroughly.

- Include the bloom hydroponic solution. It consists of sulfur, soluble magnesium, potassium, and phosphate. Then stir the mixture.

- After mixing all the nutrients in your reservoir, remember to check the pH level of the solutions. Plants wouldn't be able to adopt vital nutrients when the pH level falls outside its recommended range. Between 5.5 and 6.5 is the ideal range.

- Also, remember to check the temperature of the solutions. Too low high temperatures could lead to the death of plants. Excessively low could stun the growth of plants. Therefore, maintain 68-72 degree F.

Chapter 11: What to Grow

Now that you know what system you want to use and how to build it on a budget and have figured out where and how this system will be in your home, you're probably going to start giving serious consideration to what exactly you want to grow.

The great thing about hydroponics is that you can grow almost anything with it. Most people tend to think only of your basic herbs, like basil and thyme, but the truth is that you can grow all kinds of foods and even flowers with this system.

11.1 Food

With the hydroponics system, all kinds of food can be grown. The easiest foods to grow with a hydroponics system are:

- Artichokes
- Beans
- Lettuce
- Cabbage
- Beets
- Spinach
- Broccoli
- Asparagus
- Brussels sprouts
- Peas
- Cauliflower
- Garden peas
- Snow peas

- Snap peas
- Spinach
- Tomato
- Strawberries
- Watermelon
- Grapes
- Raspberries
- Blackberries
- Cantaloupe
- Grapes
- Blueberries
- Peppers
- Eggplant
- Cucumber
- Beans

In fact, some foods, such as beans, actually grow best in a hydroponics system as opposed to soil. There are some things that you might have to do specifically for a certain type of food in order to help it grow best.

Tomatoes, for example, grow best if you grow your first plant or two in soil and then transplant them into the hydroponics system. Other plants, such as cabbage, might need a little more space than others, and some, like broccoli, will need help in supporting the heavy stalks as they grow.

You can also grow plants that naturally grow beneath the soil, such as onions, carrots, parsnips, potatoes, leeks, radishes, and yams. However, they will probably require extra care. It's probably best to avoid them unless you are really dedicated to gardening and getting that independent, fresh, organic produce.

Some food to really avoid are plants that are built to take up a lot of space, like corn or vining plants. They'll take over your entire space, and the benefits you'd get from growing them won't outweigh the costs. But luckily, there's so much food that you can grow, you won't miss out on the few kinds that you can't!

When growing food in your hydroponics system, just like you would in any other system, you'll want to pay attention to warm weather crops versus cold weather crops. Warm weather crops are those that require warmth and a lot of sunlight that grow from April and can be harvested by late August. Some warm-weather crops are tomatoes, green peppers, eggplants, green beans, and cucumbers.

Cold weather plants, on the other hand, don't need as much warmth and can make do with weaker sunlight. You can grow them either in early spring or in early fall. Some cold-weather plants are broccoli, cauliflower, bok choy, cabbage, lettuce, spinach, Swiss chard, green onions, peas, snow peas, and sugar snaps.

Thanks to warm versus cold weather plants, you can actually have two to three harvests of crops a year, growing cold weather in early spring, warm weather throughout spring and summer, and then cold weather again in the fall. Just a little research will be necessary once you've decided what to plant, just like if you were looking to plant in the soil.

Of course, if you're growing inside and would like to try, thanks to modern technology, it is possible to attempt to grow food in the winter as well if you've got internal heating and artificial lighting. However, most would recommend that you get a good handle on growing during the three other seasons first so that you can learn through trial and error and get experience under your belt.

11.2 Herbs

These plants are probably the first ones that people think of when they hear about hydroponics. Herbs are small, don't take up a lot of room, and are easy to grow, and you don't need a large crop in order to have a good amount to use in your home.

Nearly every herb can be grown with a hydroponics system, but some examples are:

- Anise
- Basil
- Catnip
- Chamomile
- Chervil
- Thyme
- Rosemary
- Sage
- Tarragon
- Parsley
- Watercress
- Oregano

- Lavender
- Mint
- Dill
- Fennel
- Marjoram
- Cilantro
- Coriander
- Chives
- Cannabis

If you're going to be growing cannabis, of course, then you'll want to look into the regulations of wherever you live so that you're not breaking the law.

Cannabis and some of the other herbs on this list can grow very quickly — quicker than most people expect — and so you'll want to be prepared to do some trimming to keep that growth to a minimum, so it doesn't take over your entire system. But now you'll have herbs for your house, for your food, and even for medicine, as many are used in natural healing methods.

If you're someone who loves natural healing methods and relies upon them, then an herb garden can be a way for you to save tons of money by skipping those all-natural stores and just brewing your own herbal teas and such at home.

11.3 Flowers

Most people actually don't really think of flowers when it comes to hydroponics.

This is most likely because since its beginning in 1929, people have been looking at hydroponics as a way to grow crops without the use of soil, so that people can be fed, and the population can continue to survive even if the soil deteriorates or we run out of farmland thanks to city growth.

However, just because that's what most people use it for, it doesn't mean that you can't use part or all of your hydroponics system to grow flowers.

It's a lovely way to fill your apartment with beauty, and even if you use flowers as a part of your business, such as a florist, it can be a way to grow extra flowers and increase your income.

Thanks to modern technology such as indoor heating and lighting, and the fact that there are flowers that grow even in the winter, you can grow flowers year-round, unlike vegetables and herbs where you might have to wait out the winter.

Nearly any flower can be grown using the hydroponics system, just like with herbs, but some examples are:

- Petunias
- Zinnias
- Snapdragons
- Baby's breath
- Daisies
- Azania's
- Marigolds

- Coreopsis species
- Brachycome species
- English ivy
- Peace lilies
- Dracaena plants
- Philodendron
- Golden pathos
- Coleus
- Carnations
- Orchids

Let your imagination run wild and start growing the food and flowers you want today, bringing a little bit of nature into your home.

Chapter 12: Mistakes to Prevent

Even though growing hydroponic plants, the majority of the growers perpetrate exactly the exact same common mistakes that destroy their whole garden. With appropriate research and preparation, you can stay away from several such frequent mistakes. Among the biggest mistakes growers normally commit is they begin growing hydroponics plants with no fundamental understanding about ways to raise and care for hydroponically grown crops.

One common mistake the majority of the anglers perpetrate is not to offer enough air movement within their ancestral backyard. Air movement is essential to crops' breathing because it supplies fresh air to your leaf zone. The atmosphere in your living room must include enough oxygen, CO_2, but it ought not to comprise molecules of industrial pollutants, including particulates and other airborne debris. Good ventilation is essential to acquire larger returns in hydroponic gardening, but you simply cannot throw a buff on your hydroponic grow space. You want to place an ideal size enthusiast as hydroponics lovers are a significant part of your indoor garden set up and assist in handling heat, airflow, and other ecological problems. If you're utilizing HID grow to light, ventilation becomes much more significant due to the quantity of warmth these lights create. Never forget to keep the enthusiast in continuous movement, and it ought not to blow right on the plants since this may lead to dehydration.

Hydroponics plants thrive in sterile and well-maintained surroundings, and that means you ought to clean all of the debris such as fallen leaves, soil, and other substances that could attract and strain diseases. You have to keep your grow area dry to avert any sort of mold infestation. Don't smoke, consume, or even let pets close to the crops because these can offer harm to your crops.

To steer clear of these common errors in your own garden, you have to pay a close eye on your crops each day to make sure your backyard is operating smoothly. Every single time you come to your backyard, don't forget to look at your pump systems, reservoirs, water levels, pH, nutrients, lighting, plants, and timers.

If you are just starting with your hydroponic nursery, then you have to take things medium and easy. 1 misstep can conquer all of the progress you have made in your own development. Instead, place aside the attempt to understand what your crops expect from you and also the terms they want.

Numerous problems can arise in a daybed, but below are the 5 most most-regular botches that a hydro planter could cause:

12.1 Misstep 1 -- Ignoring pH Levels

The most significant estimation of your hydroponic frame is the pH level. Normally, your crops exist predominantly due to a nutritional supplement arrangement. On the off possibility that the arrangement is too antacid or too acidic, your crops will experience supplement lacks or simply bite the dust.

Get a first course pH meter and monitor the amounts at any speed once daily. On the off probability, it slides toward a route, finds a means to make it more in the parity that your crops need.

A Topsy turvy pH degree is among the most frequently recognized reasons for plants to bite the dust in a hydroponic frame. It is extremely crucial to display pH levels because each one of your crops resides at an identical supplement structure -- if your pH is bad for a single plant, then each one of your crops could survive!

12.2 Misstep 2 -- Purchasing Cheap, Wrong or Not Enough Lighting

Placing resources to the right lighting may signify the moment of fact, your hydroponic nursery! On the off probability that you buy almost nothing, your crops will survive. In the event you buy an inappropriate type of bulb to your crops, they will not grow. On the off probability that you pick to buy the cheapest bulbs, they might not perform.

Lighting is among the most critical speculations you will create as a hydroponic manufacturer, so look for the most appropriate for your own harvest! This means you ought to inquire into the kind of lighting that your plants will need about the grounds that many bulbs set out different energy kinds.

Additionally, do not expect your crops must prosper on the off probability they're set along with a window. That light is often not adequately capable of fueling the overpowering growth you expect out of a plant that is nearby.

12.3 Misstep 3 -- Using the Incorrect Plant Food

It tends to lure to obtain a bag of compost from the local nursery community to be used on your hydroponic frame. After all, it is tied in with supplements, is not that so?

Perhaps not really! Conventional manure may well not weaken completely throughout your frame. In like fashion, it may block tubes and cleanses. Instead, put funds into compost meant for hydroponic frameworks. Hydroponic compost that can be available as fluids or granules that fulfills the growing prerequisites you have to have in dirt or soil-light backyard by providing additional supplements your crops can somehow or some other overlook.

12.4 Misstep 4 -- Not Pay Attending to Sanitation

Attempt to not present your hydroponic nursery land an opportunity to become a garbage receptacle. Your Exercising propensities can significantly impact the soundness of the crops and your entire hydroponic frame.

Some Essential cleaning demands you ought to tackle:

• Maintaining floors dry and perfect

• Sterilizing and cleansing frame equipment

• Sterilizing and cleansing instruments

• Sterilizing and cleansing compartments

• Disposing of plant waste

Without genuine sanitation, it is possible to spread plant illness or contribute bothers hiding spots and sustenance.

12.5 Misstep 5 -- Deciding Not to Learn

Present hydroponic frameworks have existed since the mid-twentieth century, and at that time, a slew of information and management was made available. School courses are knowledgeable about it. Several publications are available.

Chapter 13: Pests Control

13.1 The Most Famous Nuisance Problems In Hydroponics

In case you want to control sporadically, you first will need to understand that which you might behandling. Listed below are a Part of the nuisances which you're destined to find on the off Possibility that you have bugs on your frame:

Aphids

A lot of people know about aphids from college exercises, also here you thought you're finished together. Be as it might, they really do hydroponic frameworks, especially when your crops have an inordinate quantity of nitrogen within their nutrition supply. They are usually found around the plant stalks, and these little people can be dark, green, or grayish/tan.

Whiteflies

Whiteflies may be suspicious; however, you can place them pretty efficiently. They look like little white moths (approximately 1mm long) and fly off when you are likely to receive you.

Creepy crawly Mites

Creepy crawly vermin are littler than Whiteflies, at below 1mm long. Additionally, they're definitely among the most feared pervasions of a semi-permeable frame. They do seem like slight creepy crawlies; nevertheless, since they are so modest, they could without much stretch passing see before an invasion will get far mad.

Organism Gnats

Organism gnats are just another precarious vermin because the developed gnat is not dangerous, yet the hatchlings are still. You will find the insect hatchlings ingestion at origins, which may expedite bacterial infections until long.

Thrips

Thrips, like aphids, can turn leaves yellowish or Darker in light of how they suck on the nutrition's out. They are marginally more affordable at 5mm, however, at precisely the exact same time, hard to see. They will look like small, dark stains on the upper sides of leaves.

13.2 The First Stage In Hydroponic Pest Management

Vermin control may be something that you begin rehearsing within the start, along with your hydroponic frame. Basically, putting in steps that discourage bugs are going to be your primary line of a shield. Here are the Most Perfect approaches to prevent a vermin problem:

See your stickiness

A couple of bothers, like creepy crawly parasites along with organism gnats, are especially pulled into reduced stickiness and overabundance dampness in various pieces of your frame. Shielding your own stickiness from becoming overly low (half will be an adequate amount to maintain plants seem and ward off insects) can prevent a pervasion. However, it is not about your surrounding condition. Maintaining an inordinate quantity of dampness from the growing moderate can interfere bothers, very similar to expansion gnats, from consuming habitation (especially in the event you use Rockwool (they adore).

13.3 Step-by-step directions to recognize that a vermin issue

Really, despite stubborn expectations, you can, in fact, any instance have a hassle slip its way in your frame. Like every hydroponic setup, you need to study your crops for problems consistently. Having said that, you'd prefer to not confuse signs of germs with signs of distinct issues, as an instance, supplement inadequacy or illness. Here is the way to inform if your crops are undergoing germs or another illness:

Staining:

At the stage when discomforts drain the nutritional supplements from leaves (such as aphids do), you will understand that the leaves become stained and often turn a yellowish shading. This discoloration is sprinkled around minor openings the vermin feed out of, not only, for the most part, distribute on leaves.

Spots

A couple of bugs may leave a mark illustration of stains, Irrespective of whether yellow, white, dark-colored, or dim. On the off probability that you view places, confirm whether they are shops on the leaves (out of eggs, defecation, etc.), or real injury to those leaves. On the off probability that the stains scratch, you are able to all-around bet you own a bug problem.

At the stage when you find those on almost any plant, assess the leaves and stalks of distinct plants to determine the aggravation and the amount of intrusion.

Gaps from insects versus absorbs and sores:

At the stage, once you initially see a difference or rip, it will be anything but hard to create feelings.

That's the reason it is crucial to watch closely and take a look at the advantages of some openings. Copies should be really self-evident since they will appear where warmth and light sources are close crops and reveal staining around any openings or absorb.

The bugs which Are well on how to frighten hydroponic nurseries are far more 'suckers' compared to 'munches.' That suggests that the openings that they depart from profiting from crops are small, and frequently raised and surrounded by an increasingly yellowish, or whitish land.

Things to do when you've got vermin?

On the off probability that you have seen a part of this above-unwanted effects of a vermin problem, you have to get it repaired as well as rapidly. Lamentably as soon as an aggravation has progressed in, it may be tough to relieve the matter. Nuisances can undergo a hydroponic framework for an astonishing speed; therefore, once 1 plant has been affected, others will generally follow quite soon.

Chapter 14: Other Useful Resources and Information

It is truly amazing what can be found on the internet these days. Do some of your own research and read some more about hydroponics before diving in. There are other methods out there as well as plenty of ready-made systems to purchase. It is easy to look up information on any particular plant you would like to grow to find tips, pH levels, and more.

Make friends with someone at your favorite garden center. Ask around and find someone in your community who knows all about hydroponic gardening. Sometimes, a person who is available to answer questions and show things face-to-face can be really helpful. Once someone gets hooked on hydroponic gardening, they will be happy to share their knowledge with anyone ready to listen.

Here is a little bit more information about lighting in a hydroponic system. Of course, as stated, the best lighting source is the sun. Plants generally need 4 to 6 hours of direct light, plus 8 to 10 more of bright light. Make sure to place your hydroponic system accordingly. Outdoors is great, in a window is pretty good, and if these options are not available to you, then there are plenty of good lights on the market. Here are a few to look into.

14.1 T5 Fluorescent Laps

These are the cheapest lights you can buy for hydroponics, and they also run nice and cool. Just keep in mind that these lights work great for ornamental houseplants, herbs, and leafy produce such as spinach and lettuce. They can also be used for starting seedlings, cuttings, or clones.

This could be a good light to purchase for starting seeds inside and then transplanting them to your outdoor hydroponic system. These do not work well for flowering plants or fruiting vegetables; they just do not have the needed spectrum.

Here are a few other tips for using these lights. Keep them only four to six inches above the plants. Since they run cool, there is no worry that they will burn the plants. Make sure to have 40 watts per square foot of planting bed, and a good rule of thumb is one four foot tube per every two square feet of growing bed.

14.2 High-Intensity Discharge (HID) Lighting Systems

These lights are very intense and have been used in commercial greenhouses for decades. Now they are easy to acquire and provide very good results in a home hydroponics garden. HID lighting systems provide the needed spectrum for fruiting and flowering crops. It is very close to what the sun provides outside. The only downsides are that these lights are expensive and run hot.

There are two types of HID bulbs available, metal halide (MH) and high-pressure sodium (HPS). An MH light is adequate for most vegetables in all stages, but an HPS light is preferred during the flowering/fruiting stage of plants. It is preferred, but not necessary. If you can only afford one light, definitely get a metal halide. Even though these bulbs are expensive, the good news is that they last for years.

14.3 Light Emitting Diode (LED) Grow Lights

Until recently, this new lighting technology has not really been suitable for grow lights. These are a good choice now because even though they cost more upfront, use way less electricity than traditional lighting, run cool, and last a very long time. Just be careful about what you buy. There are some cheap LED setups out there that are claimed to work for growing, but often they do not have the needed spectrums for hydroponic gardens.

At the very least, buy a mid-range LED panel that is specified as a 5-band or 7-band. However, a high-end LED grow light will yield the best results. One to look into is the California Lightworks SolarSystem 550.

In addition to lighting choices, there are also a variety of options for adding nutrients to your hydroponic garden. There are 16 elements that hydroponically grown vegetables need. Carbon, hydrogen, and oxygen are taken from the air or aerated into the solution, but the other 13 need to come from a nutrient solution. These 13 are molybdenum, copper, boron, zinc, manganese, iron, chlorine, magnesium, calcium, sulfur, potassium, phosphorus, and nitrogen. There are many pre-mixed solutions on the market.

Conclusion

Hydroponics is not a hard method to grow with. In fact, it's so efficient you'll quickly see why people want to put in the extra effort to grow their plants this way. Don't be put off by all the science. In fact, if you head to your local hydroponics store, they'll be happy to give you a basic arrangement and clear up anything you're not getting.

If you're starting out, get a small system up and running first; that way, once you have the hang of the monitoring, you'll be less likely to kill an entire expensive crop.

Hopefully, you've learned a lot about the main components of hydroponics and how to get the best plants ever. Your next step is to get your system up and to run, good luck!

Lightning Source UK Ltd.
Milton Keynes UK
UKHW021849311020
372571UK00005B/525

9 789564 023564